We hear it all the time, never have people been more divided, and it's exhausting. Conflict has always been a part of the human experience. What we need are practical tools to help us through conflict. Ash, in his book, *Loving through Conflict*, identifies how Jesus resolved conflicts. What Jesus taught and modeled two thousand years ago are timeless truths needed today. You will love how Jesus teaches us to be loving through conflict.

—Kenton Beshore
Pastor Emeritus
Mariners Church, Irvine, CA

Benjamin Disraeli, former Prime Minister of England, said, "My idea of an agreeable person is one who agrees with me." Conflicts come from sharp disagreements. Even the Christian ministry is overcome with conflicts. Paul and Barnabas had to break up as a missionary team because "the contention between them was so sharp." Every month thirteen thousand pastors are forced to resign because of conflict. Seventy percent of pastors say they have no close friends. The divorce rate of pastors has been up more than 65 percent over the past forty years. The average pastor spends 20 percent of his time dealing with church conflict. What is badly needed, not only in the church but also in society, is "conflict resolution." My good friend Ash has written this important book to help churches and individuals work through their conflicts. While Ash shares some principles on conflict resolution, his focus is on how to love and treat the person you are in conflict with. He is spot-on when it comes to dealing with one of the major problems of our day.

—Ron Keller
Retired senior pastor, Christ's Church of the Valley
Founder of Teaching the Truth Ministry

Loving through CONFLICT

ASH NARAYAN, JD, MA

ISBN 979-8-88616-174-8 (paperback)
ISBN 979-8-88616-175-5 (digital)

Christian Faith Publishing
832 Park Avenue
Meadville, PA 16335
www.christianfaithpublishing.com

All Scripture references herein are from the New King James Version (NKJV) translation of the Bible, unless otherwise noted.

Printed in the United States of America

CONTENTS

ACKNOWLEDGMENTS

I am grateful to my friend and colleague Dr. Randell Turner, the founder of Transforming Families Global Initiative. Your passion to help Christian families grow better relationships is infectious. Thank you so much for your valuable feedback and input in so many areas of this book. I pray this will be another great resource to further the mission of transforming families.

My deepest appreciation to Dr. Sherman Smith for your wisdom and early editorial support that improved the overall quality of the book. A special thanks to Paul Lasley and Kyle Young for giving me the time and resources I needed to write in an otherwise challenging environment.

To my wife, Amy, and sons, Conner and Tyler, thank you from the bottom of my heart for your continued love and support. We have been through a lot as a family, and you encouraged me to pursue my career transition into ministry and my passion to write. For that, I am forever grateful.

To the team at Christian Faith Publishing, thanks for bringing your incredible talents to this finished product.

Finally, I thank my Lord and Savior, Jesus Christ, for His grace, mercies, and daily blessings including this book. All the glory to Him. Amen.

INTRODUCTION

It was another beautiful fall day in Southern California. My day started with my morning prayers, Bible reading, and walking our two dogs. As I enjoyed a light breakfast, I scrolled through the *Los Angeles Times* (I am old-fashioned and still enjoy the feeling of a physical newspaper). The front-page headlines were dominated by the upcoming presidential and congressional elections with various stories highlighting what were likely to be hotly contested races. The international news was focused on a few trade wars and escalating violence in the Middle East. Even the sports headlines on that day centered on the labor dispute heating up between the National Basketball Association owners and players' unions over the upcoming season. Knowing I had a busy day with calls, meetings, and a deadline with our publisher on some edits for an upcoming book, I put down the paper and headed to my office.

After a productive morning, I was getting ready to leave to meet a friend for lunch when I remembered to call the restaurant. I checked to see if they were still open given the recent order by California's governor closing businesses following a surge in COVID-19 virus cases. Fortunately, the restaurant was open for take-out service, and there was an adjacent outside area with tables for dining. I arrived early, and as I waited for my friend, I watched the two televisions located above the front reception, one tuned to CNN and the other to Fox News. They were both reporting on the previous night's social protests in the Pacific Northwest. There was no volume on either television but as I read the bylines and closed-captioning, I was struck by how different and politicized the reporting was by the two networks. If I didn't know better, it would appear the two networks were not covering the same event. The couple standing next to me, waiting for their take-out order, were in an animated debate over the governor's recent shutdown, each appearing to have very different opinions on the pandemic that had consumed the world for the previous nine months. As my friend and I were enjoying our lunch outside, he shared that his ministry leadership team was divided over how to manage the rollout of a new program. He was concerned that the issues were creating fractures within his team. We also discussed a mutual friend who had reached out to each of us individually regarding his recent decision to leave his Life Group because of some "irreconcilable differences" with another member of the group. While we enjoyed more uplifting discussions about our respective families, sadly we ended our lunch, praying for a couple in our church who recently announced that they were divorcing.

After sending out the revised manuscript to our publisher and completing a few calls, I was sitting in my office, reflecting on the day. I couldn't help but feel that everywhere I turned, our world was in conflict. Politics, social justice, the COVID-19 pandemic, church ministry, and marriages are just a small sample of the myriad of issues causing division across the world, in my community, and even in my church. While conflicts are inevitable and have existed since the Fall, what was troubling to me was the way Christians were managing conflicts. As the coauthor of several books on relationships and as the director of development for Transforming Families Global Initiative, a ministry focused on building healthy relationships, I felt compelled by this to study God's wisdom on relational conflict.

The centerpiece of God's creation is man, who was not just good but "very good" (Gen. 1:31). While God enjoys His relationship with man, in His wisdom, He designed man to be in a community. All throughout the Bible, God emphasizes the importance of community. The book of Ecclesiastes describes the strength of community:

> Two are better than one because they have a
> good return for their labor. If either of them falls

down, one can help the other up. But pity anyone
who falls and has no one to help them up. Also,
if two lie down together, they will keep warm.
But how can one keep warm alone? Though one
may be overpowered, two can defend themselves.
A cord of three strands is not quickly broken.
(Eccles. 4:9–12 NIV)

The idea of community comes from our sense of responsibility for each other. In the Bible, God encourages us to care for each other to ensure a thriving community. A community does not happen if each of us is only concerned with protecting our own self-interests. God is the Creator of relationships, and our relationships matter. Jesus came to teach us the importance of love and how to relate well to one another even during conflict.

At the Tower of Babel, God saw that the homogeneity of man with "one language," and one speech was not good (Gen. 11:6). So He "confused their language" and "scattered them abroad from there over the face of all the earth" (Gen. 11:7–8). Almost immediately, many different cultures began to develop Christian communities reflecting this same diversity. Naturally, the quantity and intensity of differences on issues grew both inside and between communities. While some of these conflicts resolved themselves, many evolved into major schisms that are still seen in churches and communities today. God knew when he initiated the diaspora at Babel that conflicts would ensue. In His wisdom, He would later give us Jesus to model how to live well together despite these differences.

Humans by their nature have a strong desire to be right. From a young age, we are taught to have a conviction for our beliefs, especially those ingrained in us over long periods of time. Most people are open to a correction or adjustment of a misunderstanding or a mistake of fact. For example, if I had (improperly) learned that "2+2=5" and someone empirically showed me that "2+2=4," I would thank them and graciously accept my new understanding of this fact. However, because of our strong desire to be right, most people require a lengthier and more intense process in order to change or modify a personal opinion (setting aside, for now, the obvious arguments over what constitutes facts versus opinions). A discussion of opinions requires openness and vulnerability to engage with another human both in the written and spoken word. In its most basic form, it requires a relationship.

In a way that only God the intelligent Designer of man could do, He developed our uniqueness and individuality of opinion to allow us to grow our relationships. God wants us to be in a relationship with Him and each other. Conflicts, if left unresolved, rob us of the joy that healthy relationships bring. Therefore, understanding; working through; and, sometimes but not always, resolving conflict is critical. Jesus modeled essential principles such as compassion, kindness, empathy, humility, gentleness, and patience, all of which help us face conflict.

This book is not designed as a guide on how to resolve conflict although many of the principles discussed when implemented will likely encourage conflict resolution. While conflict resolution is a laudable goal, many, if not most, conflicts will be left unresolved. Accordingly, we need to address a different reality. A world without conflict will not happen until this earth passes away, and we gloriously enter a new heaven and new earth. So until we get to heaven, conflicts will always exist.

The objective of this book is to educate Christians on how to live well with each other in and through our conflicts (even those that are unresolved). God is all about relationships, and He desires for us to affirm and grow our relationships with each other which is much more important to Him than any issues underlying a conflict. As we trust God with our relationship issues (2 Tim. 2:12) and follow Jesus's example, we can learn to love through conflict.

PART 1

Understanding Conflict

CHAPTER 1

The Anatomy of Conflict

As Travis was leaving church on a Sunday morning, he ran into his good friend Bob who shared, "I have an issue I need your input on. Can I call you in the next few days?"

Of course, Travis replied yes, but as he left, he was curious about the somber tone in Bob's request for a discussion. Bob and Travis had first met ten years earlier when their church, Lakeview, launched a brand-new discipleship program. Bob, Travis, and a few others bravely agreed to participate as a pilot group along with the church's pastors. After completing the program, several in their group had grown close during the ten-week experience, so they formed a Life Group. Bob and his wife, Sally, graciously opened their home for them to meet, and Bob assumed the group's leadership responsibilities. Because of the various leadership and ministry roles Travis had served at the church, he supported Bob as needed. The Life Group faithfully studied God's Word, served together, and more importantly shared life together for over ten years. While it had some turnover during this time, amazingly, five from the original discipleship program (and their spouses) were still together in the group. Although Travis was in a few other groups as part of his spiritual walk, this Sunday evening Life Group was the one he and his wife, Mary, valued the most.

Bob and Travis connected on Tuesday, and Bob began to describe an issue between two members of the Life Group, Diane and Carol. Diane was a successful consultant for a major company who grew up as a missionary in Europe. She was an original member of the group. She was a godly woman who studied the Bible regularly and attended Lakeview as well as two other churches in the area. Carol and her husband, Alan, joined the Life Group five years earlier after Travis and his wife, Mary, had co-led them through Lakeview's church discipleship program which, by now, almost everyone in the church had gone through. Following the program, they quickly became friends, and since Carol and Alan were new to the church, Travis and Mary introduced them to Bob and invited them to join the Life Group. Carol, a former teacher at a Christian school, had led Bible studies for over thirty years and became a key contributor to the group.

Bob shared that Carol was leading a new Bible study at Lakeview for about thirty women, and Diane and two other women from the Life Group had been attending. Bob explained that the format of the group was that Carol taught a lesson for about thirty minutes, followed by the women going into breakout groups for discussion based on flow questions that Carol had prepared. The large group would then reconvene for final comments and questions and to close in prayer.

Carol had called Bob last week, explaining to him that Diane had been "purposefully disruptive" in the large group lesson segment by interrupting her on several occasions. Carol equated this to someone interrupting a pastor while he or she preached a sermon. What further bothered Carol was that in these interruptions, Diane would often challenge Carol's theology, questioning if she was doctrinally accurate. During the small-group breakout time, Carol explained that Diane would also try to teach the other women and ignore the flow questions she had prepared. These incidents repeatedly happened over the first three weeks of this new Bible study. Carol shared that she and Alan had been praying about this, but because she had felt so disrespected by Diane's actions, they had decided to leave the Life Group.

Travis was surprised and saddened by this disclosure. But after collecting himself, since Bob had sought his input on how to best approach Diane regarding the situation, he said a quiet prayer. Bob reiterated that Carol had made it clear that she and Alan were resolute in their decision, and she had no desire to either meet with Diane or discuss this any further. However, she appreciated that Bob, as the leader of the group, had to adequately address the issue to the other group members. As Travis continued to process the facts, he asked Bob if Diane was aware of any of this, and Bob indicated he was not sure as he had yet to speak with her. They agreed that the next step would be to request Carol's permission for Bob to talk to Diane with full disclosure of Carol's feelings regarding the Bible study and her decision to leave the group. Bob received Carol's permission and called Diane a few days later.

Travis suggested to Bob that before calling Diane, he speak with the other women in the Life Group who attended the Bible study to seek their observations of the incidents. Each of them confirmed that Diane had been "overly vocal" during the Bible studies. They said this was Diane's nature given her keen interest and faithful study of God's Word. However, they seemed to appreciate Carol's frustration as they know how hard she worked to prepare for each lesson and how she felt called from a young age to teach the Bible. Finally, they were surprised and disappointed by Carol's decision to leave the group. They sensed that Carol, who typically had a steady demeanor and positive attitude, had been deeply impacted by Diane's actions and no longer wanted to be associated with her.

When Bob finally spoke with Diane, he thoughtfully recapped his conversations with Carol and the other Life Group members of the Bible study. He was careful not to have it come off as accusatory or judgmental. Diane seemed surprised by Carol's description of the "incident" and quickly began to defend her conduct. Bob reassured Diane that she was not on trial, and the purpose of the call was not to determine who was right or wrong. Fortunately, Bob was able to de-escalate the call's tone, and they had a productive discussion. They closed in prayer and agreed to talk again very soon.

Bob and Travis met for lunch a few days later. Despite his desire to meet with Carol and Alan to try to get them to reconsider their decision to leave the group, Travis committed to Bob to wait to contact them until they met. They discussed how they could care for Carol and Diane and do their best not to cause any problems going forward for the Life Group. They left their lunch with a plan that Bob would have a follow-up meeting with Diane, and Travis would talk with Carol and Alan. Before Travis had a chance to call Alan to schedule a meeting, he ran into Alan and Carol at a church function the next day. After the function, Travis asked if they had time to grab a cup of coffee, and they agreed. As they sat outside of the cafe, Travis shared that Bob had debriefed him on everything, and he was just reaching out as a friend to offer love and support for what he knew had been a painful ordeal for both. As Carol honestly shared, Travis felt the real pain she experienced as a Christian woman who tried to honor God every day of her life. He resisted the temptation to encourage them to return to the Life Group and instead just listened to her talk about her call from a young age to teach the Bible, especially to children and women. She expressed frustration with the incident and did not want to be exposed to any negative people who would disrupt her teaching at this stage of her life. Travis asked her if she would be open to meeting or talking with Diane as Christian sisters, and she respectfully declined.

When Bob met with Diane, she began the conversation by stating that she had prayed extensively about the Bible studies and did not think she had done anything wrong. Her position was that Christians should always be ready to vigorously debate theological issues, and those who choose to teach or lead need to be prepared to defend their positions. While Bob patiently let Diane complete her defense, he then pointed out that while he did not necessarily disagree with her point on the theological debate, this was about a different issue. He reminded Diane of a separate incident several years earlier when during a passionate discussion in the Life Group, how she got overly aggressive with another member, who, as a result, took a break from the group for several weeks. He emphasized that neither he nor anyone was judging her and that it was not about the theological debate but relationships and respect. He asked Diane if she would be willing to meet with Carol—she declined but did agree to email her an apology. Bob was copied on the apology but was disappointed when most of the apology was a thesis on the importance of theological debate. Only at the very end of the email did Diane provide a terse apology and well wishes.

When the Life Group met the following Sunday, Diane was not in attendance as she was traveling on business. Bob announced that Alan and Carol had decided to leave the group. While careful not to give a specific reason, he said they were spending more time in the desert (which was truthful as they owned a home in Palm Springs) and had other commitments that would cause them to miss the Sunday meetings. While Travis agreed with Bob's decision not to discuss the issue between Carol and Diane, he was saddened that close friends and vital contributors to the group had left. However, what troubled him more was he felt that the group had missed an opportunity to have a thoughtful discussion on how Christians can better manage conflict in a way that does not damage or destroy relationships.

Definition of Conflict

Webster's Dictionary defines conflict as follows:

1. to fight; battle; contend
2. to be antagonistic; incompatible or contradictory; be in opposition; clash
3. emotional disturbance resulting from a clash of opposing impulses or from an inability to reconcile impulses with realistic or moral considerations.[1]

These definitions all connote a fight or battle in which opposing viewpoints pit combatants in an aggressive posture. There is a built-in theme of hostility in these definitions. However, a biblical view of conflict tempers the harshness offered in the secular definition of conflict. A biblical view of conflict creates both a pathway to resolution and the preservation of relation-

> A biblical view of conflict creates both a pathway to resolution and the preservation of relationships.

ships. In his book, *Peacemakers*, Ken Sande offers the following definition of conflict: "a difference in opinion or purpose that frustrates someone's goal or desires."[2]

While there are some similarities between the two definitions by introducing the concepts of "opinion or purpose" as well as "goals or desires," the biblical definition emphasizes the individuals/participants as opposed to the underlying issue of the conflict.

In His creative design, God gave us free will, and in doing so, there was an expectation that we would be in conflict. Although He made us in His image, He also created each of us to be unique. Of the seven billion people on earth, no two people even have the same fingerprints. This uniqueness naturally results in differences in opinions, purposes, goals, and desires consistent with the biblical view of conflict. God is not surprised, dismayed, or overwhelmed by conflict as we often are. While God cares about the opinions, purposes, goals, and desires, He cares about us even more both as individuals and together in a community. Thus, the conflict becomes another means for Him to demonstrate His love for us and the love for each other and provides an opportunity for us to glorify Him.

> God is not surprised, dismayed, or overwhelmed by conflict as we often are.

Causes of Conflicts

The Bible is replete with stories of conflicts. Even the men and women who faithfully served God had disagreements or differences of opinions similar to those we may find in today's church. The book of Acts, which recounts the start and growth of the first-century church following the Pentecost, illustrates a conflict between the apostles Paul and Barnabas and their missionary strategy:

> Then after some days, Paul said to Barnabas, "Let us now go back and visit the brethren in every city where we have preached the word of the Lord and see how they are doing." Now

> Barnabas was determined to take with them John called Mark. But Paul insisted that they should not take with them the one who had departed from them in Pamphylia and had not gone with them to work. Then the contention became so sharp that they parted from one another. And so, Barnabas took Mark and sailed to Cyprus, but Paul chose Silas and departed, being commanded by the brethren to the grace of God. And he went through Syria and Cilicia, strengthening the churches. (Acts 15:36–41)

This exchange between Paul and Barnabas illustrates the most common cause of conflict: differences in values, goals, gifts, callings, priorities, expectations, interests, or opinions.[3] Look at the words that described Paul's and Barnabas' opinions, purposes, goals, and desires: *determined* and *insisted*. The same type of emotion was illustrated in the conflict between Carol and Diane. Because we are unique, we see things differently. We have different perspectives, and this naturally leads to conflicts, even between Christians.

Sinful attitudes and behaviors are another cause of conflict. The apostle James asks the questions, "Where do wars and fights come from among you? Do they not come from the desires for pleasure that war in your members?" (James 4:1). He goes on to articulate that sin and the problems that result from sinful behavior are causes for conflict.

Miscommunication and poor communication often lead to misunderstandings that result in conflict. This was illustrated in the book of Joshua when the children of the tribes of Reuben, Gad, and Manasseh built an altar by the Jordan (Josh. 22:9–34). While their intent was pure in building an altar to commemorate a place of remembrance celebrating God's faithfulness, it was not communicated clearly. The other tribes and leaders thought they intended to turn away from the Lord. Fortunately, the miscommunication was cleared up before the conflict escalated. Our words and actions, if not communicated clearly, can often result in unintended conflict.

While there are many other causes for conflict, an emerging trend that has created tension and division among Christians is centered on ideology. Christianity's fundamental beliefs and truths are no longer commonly accepted. Movements such as social justice and moral relativism are dominating the teaching and culture of the younger generation and academia. These movements go far beyond the Christian issues that were debated vigorously in the early church such as transubstantiation or homeostasis. They even go deeper than the significant issues that were debated in the Protestant Reformation. These progressive movements are the cause of substantial conflict among Christians who steadfastly proclaim their love for the same God. This book will not examine in detail the merits of the competing issues and interests in these progressive movements. We will focus on how God calls Christians to respond to each other in these types of conflicts as well as the different kinds of conflicts we face every day.

CHAPTER 2

God's View of Conflict

Unity, Not Uniformity

In his letter to the church in Ephesus, the apostle Paul begins to explore the Christian response to God's gracious plan of salvation. In verses one to thirteen emerges the important theme of unity:

> I, therefore, the prisoner of the Lord, beseech you to walk worthy of the calling with which you were called, with all lowliness and gentleness, with longsuffering, bearing with one another in love, endeavoring to keep the unity of the Spirit in the bond of peace. There is one body and one Spirit, just as you were called in one hope of your calling; one Lord, one faith, one baptism; one God and Father of all, who is above all, and through all, and in you all.

> But to each one, as grace was given according to the measure of Christ's gift. Therefore He says: "When He ascended on high, He led captivity captive, and gave gifts to men."

> (Now this, "He ascended"—what does it mean but that He also first descended into the lower parts of the earth? He who descended is

also the one who ascended far above all the heavens, that He might fill all things.)

And He Himself gave some to be apostles, some prophets, some evangelists, and some pastors and teachers. For the equipping of the saints for the work of ministry, for edifying the body of Christ, till we all come to the unity of the faith and the knowledge of the Son of God, to a perfect man; to the measure of the stature of the fullness of Christ. (Eph. 4:1–13)

Webster's Dictionary defines unity as the quality of being one in spirit, sentiment, or purpose.[4] It further defines unity as harmony, the state of peaceable or friendly relations.[5] The Greek translation of the command to "keep the unity" (Eph. 4:3) suggests that maintaining unity is to be a matter of the utmost importance and urgency. We are to spare no effort and make it a priority for our lives to maintain the unity of the Spirit. Such an exhortation also makes it plain that the unity of the Spirit is a reality that is to be demonstrated visibly. As Christians contribute to the unity of the church, we accomplish the blessings of salvation and respond to the divine purpose for eternal unity.

An important feature of this passage is the notion of unity in diversity. Verses seven, eleven, and twelve emphasize the diversity produced by the essential contributions of each individual man. This diversity can be a factor that promotes rather than hinders unity. Verses two, fifteen, and sixteen suggest that love is essential for achieving harmony and unity in diversity. Love means unity is more important to you than being right, having your way, or getting what you want. Love provides the perfect platform for unity.

> Love means unity is more important to you than being right, having your way, or getting what you want.

In one of his final prayers before his betrayal and arrest, Jesus emphasized the importance of unity when He declared to God the

Father His desire that "they all may be one" and that "they may be made perfect in one" (John 17:21, 23). Similar to Paul's exhortation in Ephesians 4, Jesus ties in the critical component of love in binding unity, "the love with which You loved Me may be in them, and I in them" (John 17:26).

By contrast, uniformity in the context of conflicts suggests agreement or seeing things similarly. When the goal in conflict resolution is reaching an agreement or meeting of the minds, this becomes the parties' primary motivation. While this is a laudable goal, we know from practical experience this is not always possible. When we understand that the Bible teaches that some differences of opinions, perspectives, and desires are permissible and often beneficial, it amplifies the beauty of our diversity. God does not desire or demand uniformity but demands that we work with and embrace those we may be in disagreement with.

However, one specific area where God demands uniformity among Christians is honoring the absolute truth of the Bible. True Christians are people who acknowledge and live under the Word of God. His words to us are true because God cannot lie (Titus 1:2; Num. 23:19; Heb. 6:18), which is why His words to us are true (see also Ps. 119:151). The truth claims of Christianity are not incidental to its identity; they are its identity.

Absolute truth is commonly defined as something that is true at all times and at all places. It is something that is always true, no matter what the circumstances. Fundamental to Christianity is that Christian truth is absolute in nature. This means that God's truth is invariant. It is true without exception or exemption. Neither is God's truth relative, shifting, nor revisable. Jesus clearly articulated the absoluteness of God's truth in John 14:6: "I am the way, the truth, and the life. No one comes to the Father except through me." Paul reinforced this absoluteness in 1 Corinthians 8:6: "Yet for us there is one God, the Father, of whom are all things, and we for Him; and one Lord Jesus Christ, through whom are all things, and through whom we live." Because the core of our faith is absolutely true, Christians have nothing to fear and should be open to intellectual engagement with fellow believers and non-Christians alike.

This engagement may result in conflict, but through truth in love, relationships can not only endure but also grow stronger.

Inherent in the understanding of biblical truth is the fact that God's promises are true—"He who promised is faithful" (Heb. 10:23). God demonstrates His faithfulness by His unfailing fulfillment of His promises. God never fails those who trust His Word. One source of Christian disunity in today's church is the abandonment of absolute truth. J. I. Packer writes, "These things were understood once, but liberal theology, with its refusal to identify the written Scriptures with the Word of God, has largely robbed us of the habit of meditating on the promises."[6] We are called to speak the truth in love in community with other people. Christians cannot forsake truth for relationships or forsake relationships for truth. We will examine this in more detail in part 3.

An Opportunity to Imitate Him

Therefore be imitators of God as dear children.
And walk in love, as Christ also has loved us
and given Himself for us, an offering and a
sacrifice to God for a sweet-smelling aroma.

—Eph. 5:1–2

Following the example of God in all areas of life is a recipe for success. It is especially important with respect to how we behave in a conflict where the flesh can dominate our thinking and actions. Ephesians 5:2 makes clear that Christians imitate God when they walk in His love. *Imitators,* as used here, means likeness and similarity. We are to depend on God in all of our actions and not rely on our own independent success. Our close relationship with God should be both the reason for our imitating him and the motive that prompts us. Believers have been adopted into God's family and should exhibit the family resemblance. As God's dearly

> Our love is to imitate God's love.

loved children, we live our lives out of the love we have already experienced from the Father. Our love is to imitate God's love.

Jesus taught us how to imitate God and walk in love. As we follow the Lord (1 Thess. 4:6), He provides an example in four important areas that God wants us to imitate His love when we face conflict.

1. *Humility.* We are called to "be submissive to one another, and be clothed with humility for 'God resists the proud, But gives grace to the humble'" (1 Pet. 5:5). Jesus provided the ultimate example of humility giving up the status and privilege that were His in heaven when "he did not think of equality with God as something to cling to. Instead, he gave up His divine privileges; he took the humble position of a slave" for our sake to come live as a man (Phil. 2:6–7 NLT). We demonstrate humility when we look at the interest of others (Phil. 2:4).

2. *Mercy.* Jesus regularly showed mercy to those in misery and distress, caring for the sick, the poor, and the marginalized. His example encourages us to act similarly to those we may be in conflict with. Mercy is undeserved favor, and it is a characteristic that distinguishes Christians. The parable of the Good Samaritan (Luke 10:30–37) is an excellent example of how we can imitate Jesus's mercy to others by demonstrating sympathy, kindness, and compassion to someone in need. The person we are in conflict with may often be in need.

3. *Forgiveness.* When we are in a conflict, the relationship is often at a crossroads—it can break down or be strengthened. Forgiveness is the glue that can strengthen a relationship confronted with a conflict. We imitate God when we show forgiveness to another and recognize Jesus's sacrifice on the cross. If we have unforgiveness in our hearts against someone else, then we are not acting in a way that is pleasing to God. Jesus stressed the importance of our forgiveness to others as a central characteristic of our day-to-day relationship with God (see Matt. 6:14–15 and Mark 11:25).

4. *Loving correction.* When we value relationships over being right, if faced with a matter in which we believe a Christian brother or sister may be incorrect or ensnared in sin, we can imitate God and how He lovingly corrects us. In Matthew 18:15, Jesus provides guidance on how to lovingly correct a fellow Christian you may be in conflict with: "Moreover if your brother sins against you, go and tell him his fault between you and him alone. If he hears you, you have gained your brother." Jesus provided numerous examples in which he offered loving correction as opposed to a blunt confrontation of sin or wrongful behavior, such as the Samaritan woman at the well (John 4:1–18) and the parable of the prodigal son (Luke 15:11–32).

An Opportunity to Glorify Him

God did not need to create man, yet he created us for his own glory (Isa. 43:7). While God did not need us or the rest of creation for anything, we and the rest of creation glorify Him and bring Him joy. The fact that we were created to glorify God indicates that we are important to Him. As Christians, our purpose in life must be to fulfill the reason that God created us to glorify Him. Therefore, our appropriate response is that "whatever you do, do all to the glory of God" (1 Cor. 10:31). Notice in this Scripture that the apostle Paul emphasizes "whatever you do," we are to glorify God. He does not limit the directive to when things are going well or when there is harmony in our relationships. No, he wants us to give God praise and glorify Him even when we are in conflict with another Christian. Even when we suffer, God instructs us "[to] not be ashamed, but [to] glorify God in the matter" (1 Pet. 4:16).

When in conflict, we need to follow Jesus's example who always sought to please His Father. In John 5:30, He said, "I do not seek My own will but the will of the Father who sent Me." Later, as He taught in the temple, He declared, "And He who sent Me is with Me. The Father has not left Me alone, for I always do those things that please Him" (John 8:29). Jesus glorified God in "whatever He did" by doing what pleased the Father.

David provides a great example of pleasing and glorifying God when he faced a harrowing conflict as he was pursued by King Saul who sought to kill him. In 1 Samuel 24, after multiple attempts on David's life, Saul and three thousand of his men pursued David into the Wilderness of En Gedi. Saul went into a cave to relieve himself and unbeknownst to him, David was hiding in the recesses of the cave. While David's men encouraged him to end the conflict by killing an unsuspecting Saul which he could have easily done, David knew that would not be pleasing to God. After Saul exited the cave and was at a safe distance, David announced to Saul the reason for sparing his life: "I will not stretch out my hand against my lord, for he is the Lord's anointed" (1 Sam. 24:10). Saul acknowledging David's mercy responded, "For if a man finds his enemy, will he let him get away safely? Therefore, may the Lord reward you with good for what you have done to me this day" (1 Sam. 24:19). David's compassionate response to Saul at the height of conflict pleased God and glorified Him just as Saul prophesied. God later rewarded David as He anointed him the king of Israel (see later in 1 Sam. 26:7–25 when David spares Saul's life for the second time, further glorifying God).

When we realize that God created us to glorify Him and start acting in ways that fulfill that purpose, then we begin to experience an intense joy in the Lord that we have never before known. Conflicts present a unique opportunity to please God by releasing worldly pursuits such as winning the argument and pleasing ourselves. Instead, we are called to respond to the conflict graciously, wisely, and compassionately in a way that is pleasing to God and glorifies Him.

PART 2

Understanding Relationship

CHAPTER 3

The Importance of Relationship

Webster's Dictionary defines relationship as follows:

1. the quality or state of being related; connection
2. connection by blood, marriage, etc.; kinship
3. a continuing attachment or association between persons[7]

This definition emphasizes connection and attachment. Connection and attachment are what distinguish the strength of a relationship. We may have a relationship with someone who was a classmate in school or whom we worked with because we share a common connection. However, the classmate or coworker with whom we shared continuing life experiences (i.e., attachment) grows to be a stronger relationship.

One of the most beautiful and closest relationships in the Bible was between Jonathan and David. Jonathan was the son of Saul, the king of Israel. David, the youngest son of Jesse, was a shepherd whom Saul first summoned to play a harp for him to quiet a distressing spirit that plagued him. Jonathan and David, through their common connection to Saul, forged a relationship. The relationship grew stronger to a level that when David returned from slaying Goliath the Philistine, "the soul of Jonathan was knit to the soul of David, and Jonathan loved him as his own soul"

(1 Sam. 18:1). The closeness of the relationship was described as follows:

> Then Jonathan and David made a covenant, because he loved him as his own soul. And Jonathan took off the robe that was on him and gave it to David, with his armor, even to his sword and his bow and his belt. (1 Sam. 18:3–4).

Later, when Saul began persecuting David and tried to kill him, Jonathan regularly warned David and protected him from potential attacks. Jonathan's loyalty to David continued to the very end of his life when he was killed in a battle with the Philistines. David mourned the death of his close friend as written in the Song of the Bow:

> I am distressed for you, my brother Jonathan; You have been very pleasant to me; Your love to me was wonderful, Surpassing the love of women. (2 Sam. 1:26)

Many years after Jonathan's death, David, who was now the king of Israel, honored the memory of his dear friend by caring for his lame son, Mephibosheth. Even years later when the Lord ordered King David to kill seven descendants of Saul, he spared Mephibosheth "because of the Lord's oath that was between them, between David and Jonathan" (2 Sam. 21:7).

> The overflow of God's love into our relationship with others is the foundation of Christian relationships. The strength of this foundation determines the strength of our relationships to carry us through conflicts.

The strength and closeness of Jonathan and David's relationship began with the strength and closeness of each of their respective relationships with God. A relationship with God begins with knowing God which is different from knowledge of God. Loving God is our response to knowing God. In turn, our relationship with others flows from our love for God. This continuum, knowing God, loving God, and the overflow of love into our relationship with others, is the foundation for understanding the importance of Christian relationships. The strength of this foundation determines the strength of our relationships to carry us through conflicts.

Made in His Image

Our relationship with God begins with the fundamental truth that we are made in His image.

Then God said, "Let Us make man in Our image, according to Our likeness… So God created man in His own image; in the image of God He created him; male and female He created them" (Gen. 1:26–27).

The Hebrew word for *image* (*tselem*) and the Hebrew word for *likeness* (*demut*) refer to something that is similar to the thing it represents or is an image of. As image bearers, we are similar to and represent some of God's qualities such as moral, ethical, and intellectual abilities. The cognitive abilities and emotions God blessed man with give us a unique ability to relate to God and others.

From the beginning, God our Father, God the Son, and God the Spirit (the Trinity) were in perfect relationship with each other and in perfect relationship to creation. As image bearers, man is God's representative on earth. God desires us to be in fellowship and harmonious relationship with each other as modeled by the Trinity. The more we know about God, the more similarities we will recognize including those qualities necessary for strong relationships.

Knowing God

Thus says the LORD:
Let not the wise man glory in his wisdom,
Let not the mighty man glory in his might,
Nor let the rich man glory in his riches;

> But let him who glories glory in this,
> That he understands and knows Me.

—Jer. 9:23–24

John 17:3 states, "And this is eternal life, that they may know You, the only true God, and Jesus Christ whom You have sent."

In these two scriptures, God the Father and God the Son declare that knowing God may be the single most important aspect of being a Christian. The source of our joy and sense of importance ought to come not from our own abilities or possessions but from the fact that we know Him (and His Son). However, *knowledge of* God (knowing God) is more important than *knowledge about* Him.

A thorough study and understanding of theology and the ability to think clearly and talk well on different Christian subjects may signify deep knowledge *about* God but is not the same as *knowing* Him. Similarly, we may be the model of Christian living in our prayer, worship, and church life and not know God. Jesus hated pure religion, often condemning the Pharisees who reveled in ceremony and pretense (see Matt. 23). Although they knew the law and studied the Scriptures, they did not know God, thus the critical distinction between knowing facts about God and knowing God and developing a personal relationship with Him.

Knowing God is not a mechanical step-by-step process. It is a lifetime pursuit that requires regular, if not daily, commitment. When we understand and appreciate that God desires a personal relationship with us and communicates with us regularly in many different ways, we can begin to understand how we come to know God. In his Christian classic, *Knowing God*, J. I. Packer outlines four activities in our relationship with God as we seek to know Him:

1. We listen to God's Word and receive it as the Holy Spirit interprets it in application to oneself.
2. We note God's nature and character as His Word and works reveal it.
3. We accept His invitations and do what He commands.

4. We recognize and rejoice in the love that He has shown in approaching us and drawing us into His divine fellowship.[8]

Knowing God is much more than an intellectual experience. It requires the transformation of our heart. Those who know God have great energy for God and desire to do His will.[9] The prophet Daniel writes, "The people who know their God shall be strong, and carry out great exploits" (Dan. 11:32). This energy and strength magnify us in all areas of our life—most notably in our care for others and, as Daniel demonstrated, in our prayers and worship to God.

Those who know God also have great thoughts of God. While in our finite capacities as humans, we will never know the full nature of His sovereignty or mercy toward us. Those who know God meditate and rejoice in His greatness (Ps. 145:5–6); His understanding (Ps. 147:5); His knowledge (Ps. 139:6); and His riches, wisdom, judgments, and ways (Rom. 11:33). Those who know God show great boldness for God. When we know God, we have a loyalty to Him that moves us to boldly follow Him. When we know Him, "we ought to obey God rather than men" (Acts 5:29), and we do so with passion and spirit. Finally, those who know God have great contentment in God: "Godliness with contentment is great gain" (1 Tim. 6:6). Our knowing God is never a completed task; hence, Paul's prayer and exhortation for the church in Colossae that they be ever "increasing in the knowledge of God" (Col. 1:10).

Knowing Jesus

The apostle John reminds us that to know God, we must know Jesus who is himself God manifest in the flesh:

> I am the way, the truth, and the life. No one comes to the Father except through Me. If you had known Me, you would have known My Father also. (John 14:6–7)

Knowing Jesus is in many ways easier than knowing God because He lived among man and allowed himself to be known through the earthly life He lived. The lessons taught by Jesus throughout the Gospels provide the truth about His deity. Our response to His atoning sacrifice is to make Him the Lord of our lives.

To Know Jesus, a person's whole lifestyle, value system, speech, and attitude are marked by surrendering to Christ as Lord of your life. When Jesus called people to follow Him, He was calling people to yield completely and unreservedly to His lordship. Contemporary Christians have been conditioned to believe that because they recited a prayer, signed on a dotted line, walked an aisle, or had some other experience, they are saved and should never question their salvation.[10] However, justification without sanctification is not real salvation. A sign of our faith is our obedience. "For as the body without the spirit is dead, so faith without works is dead also" (James 2:26).

Jesus warned us that the cost of following Him is high:

> Not everyone who says to Me, "Lord, Lord," shall enter the kingdom of heaven, but he who does the will of My Father in heaven. Many will say to Me on that day, "Lord, Lord have we not prophesied in Your name, cast out demons in Your name, and done many wonders in Your name?" And then I will declare to them, "I never knew you; depart from Me, you who practice lawlessness!" (Matt. 7:21–23).

It does not get much clearer than Jesus's statement in verse 23: "I never knew you." To know Jesus requires obedience to His teaching. Implicit obedience to His commandments is the necessary, expected, and natural fruit of genuine love for Him.[11] To know Jesus is to not just believe in Him but to follow Him.

When we know Jesus and trust Him to guide our lives, He declares, "I know them, and they follow Me. And I give them eternal life, and they shall never perish; neither shall anyone snatch them out of My hand" (John 10:27–28). When we know the Father and the Son, we are transformed, and our hearts open to respond in love.

Our Response—Loving God

Hear, O Israel: The LORD our God, the LORD is One!
You shall love the LORD your God with all your heart,
with all your soul, and with all your strength.

—Deut. 6:4–5

As Moses prepared the people of Israel to enter the Promised Land, he offered this statement and command linking their knowledge of God to the natural and required response: loving God. The Hebrew word for *one* used in verse four is *echad* which conveys the idea of one as a group. This was intended as a direct reference to God as one—one in Father, one in Son, and one in Spirit. Other translations of verse four read, "The Lord alone" (that is the only one). In other words, Moses is saying, "Hear, O Israel, and come to know Him as your only God."[12]

Just as we come to know God and grow in our love for Him, our relationship with others will benefit from the same process. *Philia* is the Greek word that describes the love between friends. The Christian life allows these types of relationships to flourish.

This friendship love begins to form when common insights and interests create an initial bond that grows stronger as we open up and share and get to know each other better. It requires a willingness to want to know each other at a deeper level. Christian friendship that is sourced and nourished from the overflow of God's love is powerful and as God intended. C. S. Lewis in *The Four Loves* describes this as follows:

This love [friendship], free from instinct,
free from all duties but those which love has
freely assumed, almost wholly free from jealousy,
and free without qualification from the need to

be needed, is eminently spiritual. It is the sort of
love one can imagine between angels.[13]

As we seek to know each other, we develop deep durable
relationships that imitate God's love. An *eros* love similar to that
between a husband and wife or in which Christ is represented as the
Bridegroom of the Church. Lewis offers that friendship that resembles the love between God and man rises to "the highest love of all."[14]

Our relationships with others, when founded in God's love, will
be like a house built on rock. "[When] the rain descended, the floods
came, and the winds blew and beat on that house; and it did not fall,
for it was founded on the rock" (Matt. 7:25). Conflicts are the rain,
floods, and wind. Strong relationships have the ability to endure conflicts with love as the foundational rock.

CHAPTER 4

Relationship Disciplines

As our love for God overflows into our relationships with others, these relationships will grow stronger. Love is the guiding force to sustain healthy relationships. However, God has graciously provided us with great additional wisdom that will both allow our relationships to flourish and build durability to withstand potential conflicts.

Our book *Relationship Foundations*, outlines key fundamental principles taught and modeled by Jesus that are critical to healthy relationships. In addition to several of these principles, we have added a few other principles that are critical disciplines when facing potential conflicts. Through Jesus's guidance, these relationship disciplines provide us with excellent examples and essential skills to help us improve our relationships with Him and each other.[15]

> God has graciously provided us with great wisdom that will both allow our relationships to flourish and build durability to withstand potential conflicts.

Communication

When Jesus had finished saying these things, the crowds
were amazed at his teaching, because he taught as one who
had authority, and not as their teachers of the law.

—Matt. 7:28–29 (NIV)

Communicating well is one of the most essential skills in life. It
is vital to all healthy relationships. God desires communication with
us through both prayer and worship. God created communication
and gave extraordinary powers to words and language. As noted in
Matthew 7, Jesus communicated with grace and compassion but also
with conviction and belief. The apostle Paul's instruction on communication says, "Be gracious in your speech. The goal is to bring
out the best in others in a conversation, not put them down or cut
them out" (Col. 4:6 MSG). Words that come out of our mouths
have their sources in the thoughts of our hearts. When our heart
is properly focused on the Lord, in fellowship with the Father, and
being led by the Spirit, our words will be gracious (always in truth),
uplifting, and helpful.

To have effective communication, both parties must understand how the other feels. The hallmarks of good communication
are as follows:

1. We speak directly to the person (not through them).
2. Our message is clear.
3. We are respectful; we show care and concern for the other
   person.

When communicating, it is important to use "I" statements and
reflective listening. It is not just about communicating the content of
the message but the feelings associated with the message.

Effective listening is also a critical component of communication. We should not only hear what the other person has to say but
also listen to the emphasis and understand the meaning and emo-

tions behind the words being conveyed. Several proverbs provide wisdom on the importance of effective listening:

> Fools find no pleasure in understanding but delight in airing their own opinions. (Prov. 18:2 NIV)

> Stop listening to my instruction, my son, and you will stray from the words of knowledge. (Prov. 19:27 NIV)

> Like an earring of gold or an ornament of fine gold is the rebuke of a wise judge to a listening ear. (Prov. 25:12 NIV)

We are responsible for every word we say. Words can injure people as well as build them up. Words are powerful, and we need to use words wisely. "A word out of your mouth may seem of no account, but it can accomplish nearly anything (or) destroy it" (James 3:3–5 MSG). What we say is directly correlated to the condition of our heart. Luke echoed this truth when he wrote, "A good man brings good things out of the good stored up in his heart, and an evil man brings evil things out of the evil stored up in his heart. For the mouth speaks what the heart is full of" (Luke 6:45 NIV). When we abide in Christ and are filled with the Holy Spirit, we communicate in a way that glorifies God. Remember, we all have a strong need for community and belonging. Effective communication is not just about speaking and listening; it is about connecting at a deeper level with another human being.

Honesty

I am the way and the truth and the life.

—John 14:6 (NIV)

God made honesty one of His commandments: "You shall not give false testimony of your neighbor" (Exod. 20:16 NIV). Honesty is more than just being truthful; it is about moral character. As noted above in John 14, Jesus is not only true but Truth itself. This includes His person and character. Honesty is a direct reflection of your inner character. Your actions are a reflection of your faith, and reflecting the truth in your actions is a part of being a good witness.

Honesty is mandatory for a healthy relationship. We are free to be ourselves when we find ourselves in relationships where we can be honest. This openness (see below) allows for full and complete discussions and growth in the relationship. Honesty is about sharing the truth in a way that the other person will hear and benefit from it. Honesty needs to be tender (see below on sensitivity). Truth and love are fused together. If love is not attached to honesty in our relationships, it is not love. To have the kind of deep intimate relationships we desire, honesty must become a way of life and not just a behavior.

Openness/Transparency

While honesty is a critical discipline for a healthy relationship, and if we are reluctant to address challenging issues or behavior for fear of experiencing pain, the relationship will never flourish.

> Open rebuke is better than love carefully concealed. Faithful are the wounds of a friend, but the kisses of an enemy are deceitful. (Prov. 27:5–6)

This Scripture exhorts Christians in close relationships (see friendship love in chapter 3) to rebuke each other openly and tell each other things they need to hear, even if it is painful. Verse six stresses that anyone afraid to honestly share what needs to be said does not value the relationship. It goes to the extreme of characterizing such a person as an "enemy." The benefit of honest rebuke is captured in Psalm 141:

> Let the righteous strike me;
> It shall be a kindness.
> And let him rebuke me;
> It shall be as excellent oil;
> Let my head not refuse it.
> For still my prayer is against the deeds of the
> wicked. (Psalm 141:5)

David expresses his willingness to not only accept the rebuke from the righteous (someone whose relationship he values) but also equates it to an act of kindness. When we are open and transparent in our closest relationships, we help our friends gain perspectives we often cannot see on our own. We shine a light on blind spots, a reflective light that can often help the other person understand and improve a weakness or correct sinful behavior.

Many Christians are afraid to be open and transparent, fearing that doing so may cause conflict that will damage the relationship. They choose instead to deny the concern, issue, or behavior they experience with their friend. This results in a relationship that stays at a surface and unhealthy level. They choose to only affirm each other and discuss strengths while never addressing weaknesses. Proverbs 29:5 warns us that "a man who flatters his neighbor spreads a net for his feet." Transparency is challenging, but our relationships will grow stronger and deeper, not weaker, when we openly share with each other.

Jesus modeled openness and transparency in His relationships with His disciples. In Mark 14, the disciples were critical of Mary who poured expensive oil on Jesus to anoint His body for burial. They believed Mary should have sold the oil and given the money to the poor. Jesus quickly rebuked them, explaining that He wanted people to give freely of their own volition. While Jesus appreciated the disciples' concern for the poor for whom He had unfailing compassion, He made clear that no one should criticize another's gift, for only God can read the heart of the giver. Jesus's rebuke helped the disciples with their blind spots that they could not otherwise see.

Sensitivity

Honest, open, and transparent communication is most effective when we are emotionally connected to the other person. A lack of sensitivity, as illustrated in the following proverbs, is not only unloving but also will cause problems when faced with a conflict:

> Like the one who takes away a garment on a
> cold day, or like vinegar poured on a wound, is one
> who sings songs to a heavy heart. (Prov. 25:20 NIV)
> He who blesses a friend with a loud voice,
> rising early in the morning, It will be counted a
> curse to him. (Prov. 27:14)

Christians in strong relationships should tie their hearts to one another. If a situation requires honest and direct communication, we must "comfort the fainthearted, uphold the weak, [and] be patient with all" (1 Thess. 5:14). Isaiah 49:15 provides the poignant example that God loves us more tenderly and sensitively than a nursing mother. A Christian relationship is sensitive to the emotional and spiritual health of the other person, always seeking each other's well-being and interests (Phil. 2:4). Jesus tied his heart to ours: "In all their distress he too was distressed" (Isa. 63:9 NIV) and "My joy may remain in you and that your joy may be full" (John 15:11). Similarly, when we tie our hearts to one another, this compassion provides relational strength when we face adversity.

Trust

> Whoever can be trusted with very little can also be
> trusted with much, and whoever is dishonest with
> very little will also be dishonest with much.

> —Luke 16:10 (NIV)

Trust is the central pillar supporting any healthy relationship. Trust and honesty go hand in hand as Jesus taught in the above parable in Luke 16. When we are honest with each other, we build trust. The sense of security allows both parties in the relationship to expose themselves fully without any judgment or fears. Trusting someone means that you think he or she is reliable; you have confidence in and you feel safe with the person physically and emotionally.

There are over three hundred fifty verses in the Bible on trusting in God. It is because of our faith in God that we trust Him. He is faithful to all of His promises. He has earned our trust. In our relationships, while love and forgiveness are given freely, trust is earned through actions. However, it is not an all-or-nothing proposition and is best illustrated by the Greek word for trust, *pisteu. Pisteu* expands the definition of trust from focusing on trust in facts to trust in a person or cause. *Pisteu* also contains an important endurance component that trust develops over a period of time and not in a single moment. This expanded definition of trust helps to formulate what is commonly known as the Five Levels of Trust in Relationships:

1. Connection. When we connect with someone, we start the process of building a relationship. We have the initial trust to invest in the process.
2. Caution. We start creating opportunities where we can observe this person's character in action and allow them to view the same in us. The process of building trust has started.
3. Consistency. When we observe consistency in honest words and actions from someone, we can begin to experience the deeper levels of relational intimacy that are only possible through trust.
4. Courage. While consistency is necessary, to move to the deepest levels of intimacy requires faith, courage, and taking relational risks because we feel safe and secure in the relationship.

5.   Commitment. Our courage to trust always leads to commitment in the relationship. The level of commitment will ultimately define the level of the relationship.

Strong trust always results in strong relationships. When trust is broken, it must be rebuilt. Building and maintaining trust in a relationship takes hard work and commitment.

Respect

So the last will be first, and the first will be last.

—Matt. 20:16 (NIV)

Webster's Dictionary defines respect as a feeling of admiration for someone, to hold someone in high regard, and to show consideration for someone.[16] At its core, you respect someone you are in a relationship with even if they are different from you or if you disagree with them. You cannot even have the most basic business relationship, let alone a friendship or deeper personal relationship, if you do not respect the other person or if they do not respect you. Jesus taught in Matthew 20 that we are all equal recipients of God's gifts, and therefore, we should show respect for each other.

A secular worldview would say respect is earned. The Christian worldview demonstrates God and Jesus command respect. This is clearly illustrated through three different types of relationships.

1. Respect for governmental authority

God is our supreme authority, but because He ordains and establishes government, he wants us to respect people in authority (Rom. 13:1–7). The Bible also provides examples of others in our lives whose authority we are called to respect.

In Genesis 39 to 41, Joseph respected his bosses even when he was a slave and then a prisoner, and he did his work as though he was working for God (see Col. 3:23–24).

2. A child's respect for parents

While the Bible does not directly command us to respect our parents, the idea of respect is included in the commands to honor and obey them:

> Children, obey your parents in the Lord,
> for this is right. "Honor your father and mother"
> which is the first commandment with a promise
> so that it may go well with you and that you may
> enjoy long life on earth. (Eph. 6:2–3 NIV)

Jesus always respected the authority of His Father. Jesus honored and obeyed God the Father and modeled the same respect that children should show their parents.

3. Respect between a husband and wife

God's command for respect between spouses is made clear in Ephesians 5, "The wife must respect her husband" (Eph. 5:33 NIV), and in 1 Peter, "Husbands, in the same way be considerate as you live with your wives, and treat them with respect" (1 Pet. 3:7 NIV). Marriage is a gift of God who created this unique covenant relationship. When spouses show respect for one another, they bring glory to God and the church.

As we experience God's overflowing love, we can make investments in these relationship disciplines. Through the Holy Spirit, we can honestly communicate well with each other, with openness and sensitivity. As our relationships grow, we build trust with each other founded on respect commanded by the Father and the Son. Our relationships will be stronger and ready for any challenges we may face, including those presented by the world and the forces of spiritual darkness.

CHAPTER 5

Conflict Creator—the Enemy

As we begin to develop and nurture healthy relationships that glorify God, we need to recognize that there are spiritual forces opposed to God and everything that is good. These forces have the capacity to spark conflicts, create division among Christians, and destroy relationships. While God has already secured the final victory over spiritual darkness, these forces continue to wreak havoc on unsuspecting Christians. As we learn to love each other through conflict and preserve and strengthen our relationships with our Christian brothers and sisters, we must understand this enemy and prepare ourselves against this significant obstacle.

Who Is Our Enemy?

Spiritual forces infiltrate the Christian's life through three different battlegrounds: the world, the flesh, Satan, and his demons. Each of these independently presents risks to our relationships. When these powerful forces are working together in combination, they can be lethal. However, we should not despair because God's omnipotence is more powerful than all of these forces combined.

The world, specifically the world's system of values, is the first battleground.

> Do not love the world or the things in the world. If anyone loves the world, the love of the Father is not in him. For all that is in the world— the lust of the flesh, the lust of the eyes, and the pride of life—is not of the Father but is of the world. (1 John 2:15–16)

The world is a social battlefront of values, influences, temptations, and all things that oppose God. Television, the Internet, and social media are just a few examples of the destructive forces on relationships, causing relational conflict. Christians are tempted to have more excitement in the things of the world than they do in the things of God. The world's influence has slowly seeped into the church, the body of believers, distorting the truth and creating relational tension.

> The world's influence has slowly seeped into the church, the body of believers, distorting the truth and creating relational tension.

The second battleground is our sin nature sometimes referred to in the Bible as our "flesh."

> For I know that in me (that is, in my flesh) nothing good dwells; for to will is present with me, but how to perform what is good I do not find. For the good that I will to do, I do not do; but the evil I will not to do, that I practice. Now if I do what I will not do, it is no longer I who do it, but sin that dwells in me. (Rom. 7:18–20)

The flesh is our natural inclination toward sin that every human being inherits from Adam. Every part of our being is affected by sin—our intellects, our emotions and desires, our hearts (the center of our desires and decision-making processes), and our goals and motives. We bring this internal struggle with sin into each and every one of our relationships.

The third battle is with Satan, the supernatural ruler of this world (John 14:30) and the source of evil (Matt. 6:13). Satan and his allies use the world and flesh to influence and deceive us from doing the will of God. The apostle Peter offers a strong warning to the early Christians about Satan:

> Be sober, be vigilant, because your adversary
> the devil walks about like a roaring lion, seeking
> whom he may devour. (1 Pet. 5:8)

> Our close Christian relationships bring glory to God and are attractive targets for Satan.

Peter's imagery of a "roaring lion" means that Satan is cunning and cruel. He attacks when least expected and desires to completely destroy his prey. Our close Christian relationships bring glory to God and are attractive targets for Satan.

The Enemy's Objectives—Create Conflict and Destroy Relationships

Chris and Julie have been in a committed relationship for the past two years. They are both Christians and were baptized together after attending a Christian retreat their freshman year in college. Chris is very outgoing and has lots of friends. He spends significant time on social media and hanging out with his college buddies. Julie is more introverted and recently decided to distance herself from friends and family as she concentrates on school and prepares to graduate college. She recently received a national scholastic award at a ceremony attended by her parents and Chris. Julie's parents were understandably very proud of her and even had an article published in the local newspaper about Julie receiving her award. However her mother, who is not a Christian, used the occasion to voice her continued displeasure with Chris and reiterate to Julie that "she is way too good for him, and she can do a lot better." Although Chris and Julie attend the same church and Life Group, both have been so busy with school and other commitments that they have not been attending either as frequently as they like.

Chris has also been focused on his postcollege career planning and has been reading several blogs and talking in chat groups about money-making business opportunities. In addition, he began watching a new reality television show with his friends that regularly portrays unwholesome content. Julie's new roommate is gay and has been very critical of Julie's Christianity and her church. Julie wants to be nice to her and have a comfortable living environment, so she avoids reading her Bible at home and retreats when the subject of religion comes up. As a result of these recent life changes, Chris and Julie have experienced some recent challenges in their relationship.

During a recent dinner, Chris and Julie got into an argument. Chris had bought a new expensive watch which he proudly showed off, but Julie questioned the wisdom of such a lavish expenditure.

Chris reacted with sharp criticism of Julie never being on time saying, "So what do you know about watches?"

Chris uncharacteristically muttered a few profanities to which Julie responded with a sharp request to stop cursing and quoted James 3:6, "The tongue is a fire, a world of iniquity."

Chris did not relent, rebuking Julie for being a hypocrite for quoting Scripture but not being "Christian enough" to read her Bible at home or defend her faith or church with her roommate.

Julie got the last word by saying, "Perhaps my mother was right."

The evening would end abruptly. Chris and Julie were growing farther apart from each other, and they both knew it.

The next day Chris went out with friends, thinking this would help him forget about the previous night. As he returned home, he was a little disoriented from overindulging and hit a pole in his parking garage, causing significant property damage to his car. Julie locked herself at home, crying and mired in guilt for being a terrible Christian woman. Neither of them attended church that Sunday or their Life Group.

Chris and Julie's recent relationship problems illustrate the spiritual battlegrounds of the world, the flesh, and Satan. It is in these battlegrounds where conflicts are created and relationships destroyed. Even though both Chris and Julie knew God, love Him, and love each other, these forces subtly and powerfully crept into their relationship.

The world's influence on Chris can be seen through his increased use of social media and television. In and of themselves, these platforms are not evil. However, Chris has been seduced by the lust of the eyes (covetousness or materialism) and the lust of the flesh (sinful sensual pleasures) that has distanced him from God. Julie's behavior appears to be an example of pride in life (being proud of one's position in the world) as the recent scholastic award and platitudes from her parents and others have also distanced her from God.

Even though Chris and Julie are faithful followers of Jesus, their respective sin natures were exposed during their argument. The conflict Paul described in Romans 7 is the battle between the flesh, the part of the believer in which there is nothing good, and the will, which is the desire to do good. Sin separates us from God and each other. Chris and Julie's sinful nature created high emotion and hardened hearts, resulting in poor relationship disciplines. They did not communicate well. While they may have communicated honestly, it clearly lacked sensitivity, and they spoke disrespectfully to each other. Neither Chris nor Julie intended to hurt each other, but their flesh drew them away from following God that evening.

Satan's strategy is to deceive and destroy, and his primary tactics are temptation and accusation. Satan tempts us, convincing us that the sinful behavior "isn't so bad, it won't hurt," and assures us no one will find out and that God will forgive us anyway. Satan persists by telling us that what he is tempting us to do will actually satisfy us which can weaken our convictions so we don't care. Our thinking and decision-making become so twisted that we cannot discern right from wrong. Following Chris and Julie's argument, Satan skillfully convinced Chris that a night of drinking would not hurt him. Chris's poor decisions that followed were also a thoughtful part of Satan's plan.

Once we have sinned, Satan piles on accusations, keeping us mired in guilt and shame and attempting to alienate us as effective warriors for Christ. Satan is the father of lies (John 8:44) who wants to separate us from God and the truth of His Word. As Julie continues to withdraw and retreat from her Christian community, Satan will occupy her captive thoughts, building shame and often providing more relational hostility.

Spiritual Protection to Defend against and Stand Up to the Enemy

Fortunately, we are not in this spiritual battle alone.

> Finally, my brethren, be strong in the Lord and in the power of His might. Put on the whole armor of God, that you may be able to stand against the wiles of the devil… Therefore take up the whole armor of God, that you may be able to withstand in the evil day, and having done all, to stand. (Eph. 6:10–11, 13)

The opening exhortation in verse ten reminds Christians of their position of strength—in the Lord—and the source of strength—His power. Our relationship with Jesus (refer back to chapter 3, "Knowing God") gives us access to this power. As noted earlier, the decisive victory has already been won by God through Christ on the cross, and the task of believers is not to win but to "stand"—that is to preserve and maintain what has been won.[17] All the resources are available to us for successful resistance. These resources are divine as a spiritual battle requires spiritual weapons.

1. The belt of truth (Eph. 6:14a)

God is the source of all truth, and God's truth is absolute, eternal, and unchanging. The foundation of spiritual, moral, and relational truth comes from the Bible. When you follow God's Word (the Bible), you can distinguish what is true from what is untrue.

2. The breastplate of righteousness (Eph. 6:14b)

To be righteous means to obey God's commandments and live in a way that is honorable to Him. Righteousness is a gift from God based on Christ's work on our behalf. Being covered with the breastplate of righteousness portrays a lifestyle of trusting obedience to God.

3. The gospel of peace (Eph. 6:15a)

When we believe the truth of God's Word and trust Him, then we have the personal, inner peace that enables us to keep our footing in the daily spiritual battle. God promises us eternal life, guidance in our daily lives, and peace in the midst of pain. Trusting in these promises answers our greatest fears.

4. The shield of faith (Eph. 6:16)

The shield of faith portrays a life of protection based on faith in God's character, Word, and deeds. We have to deliberately choose faith in all circumstances. We can do so not because of blind belief but because of who God is and His promises. This shield covers the believer from head to toe during spiritual warfare.

5. The helmet of salvation (Eph. 6:17a)

The helmet of salvation portrays a lifestyle of hope that comes from focusing on our ultimate salvation. This salvation has three dimensions: our past (we are forgiven and cleansed of our sins), our present (every day we are delivered from the power of sin), and our future (our eternal reward in heaven).

6. *The sword of the Spirit (Eph. 6:17b)*

The sword of the spirit is the Word of God (i.e., the Bible) and has both offensive and defensive capacities. The sword is used defensively by applying God's Word to every doubt, temptation, and discouragement hurled at us by Satan. The sword is used offensively to cause change, and encourage spiritual growth through evangelism, teaching, preaching, and counseling.

7. *Prayer (Eph. 6:18)*

Prayer is perhaps the most crucial weapon in the spiritual battle against Satan. God is the Commander in the battle. When we connect with Him through prayer, we demonstrate our active dependence on Him and grow our relationship with Him. The spiritual forces that invaded Chris and Julie wreaked havoc on them both individually and in their relationship. Without the armor of God, Chris and Julie were defenseless against a crafty and powerful enemy.

As Chris was reading blogs, perusing social media, and watching unwholesome television programs, the breastplate of righteousness could have pointed him to God's commandments contrary to these pursuits. Armed with the belt of truth, Julie could have had confidence in pursuing and discussing the truth of the Bible in a loving way with her roommate. The shield of faith could have covered them both against the enemy's attacks that provoked and intensified their dinner argument.

However, even when the spiritual forces of the world, flesh, and Satan knock us down, God is faithful, and He and His tools are still available to lift us up. The gospel of peace can quiet Chris's and Julie's hearts and enable them to think clearly and regain their footing. The helmet of salvation can cleanse them of their sin and empower them against further attacks. As Chris and Julie study God's Word, reconnect with their church and Life Group, and pray, they can restore and strengthen their relationship. The forces of spiritual darkness may have claimed an initial victory, but if Chris and Julie persevere with relationship discipline and place God and Jesus in the center of their relationship, He will deliver them through this storm.

PART 3

Loving through Conflict

Conflicts are unavoidable. As human beings, we are passionate and often have strong convictions. We regularly disagree with others, even those with whom we are in close relationship and share a common faith.

> Where do wars and fights come from among you? Do they not come from your desires for pleasure that war in your members? You lust and do not have. You murder and covet and cannot obtain. You fight and war. (James 4:1–2)

James explains that conflicts come from the "passions" that wage war in our hearts. At its core, the conflict is a heart problem. Rather than my heart being ruled by God and motivated by God's honor, my heart is ruled by my wants, needs, and feelings. Fortunately, this is the same heart that has the capacity to look at others' interests ahead of our own and the same heart that loves others the way God loves us. So when we position our heart properly while we will not avoid or resolve all conflicts, we can undoubtedly love through the conflict.

Part 3 will examine four different conflict scenarios and demonstrate how despite a conflict in the relationship, there is a path that will lead to relationship strengthening, relationship preservation, or relationship restoration. All four of the scenarios will generally follow the assumptions/principles covered in part 2:

- The individuals involved in the conflict are Christians who desire healthy relationships.
- There is an understanding of the importance and application of the relationship disciplines of effective communication, honesty, openness and transparency, sensitivity, trust, and respect.
- There is a keen respect and appreciation of the forces of spiritual darkness and an understanding that the enemy will be working to divide and destroy the relationship.

The reality is that despite our best intentions, and even when we are practicing healthy relationship fundamentals and keeping the enemy at bay as best we can, conflicts may or may not be resolved. However, if we properly learn to approach our conflicts regardless of the outcome, love can sustain the relationship. Love is relationship glue.

CHAPTER 6

Resolving a Conflict in Love—the Relationship Is Strengthened

Jen was excited when her close college friend, Trish, called her to share that she was relocating with her family to Smalltown. Trish's husband received a promotion and an opportunity to head the local office. Trish's children, who were almost exactly the same age as Jen's children, would be enrolling in time for the new school year. Jen's kids, who were close to Trish's kids from all the family vacations they had spent together, texted them with details about the school, clubs, sports, and how they would help them get connected. Trish and her husband were relieved and so thankful that one of their biggest concerns, their kids having to adjust to new friends and a new school, was likely not going to be an issue.

On Trish's last scout trip before their move, she stayed at Jen's home. Jen showed her around the neighborhood, and they had lunch with the women's pastor at Jen's church. Trish immediately connected with her and was confident her family had found a new church home to worship. As Trish was getting ready to leave for the airport the next morning, Jen's long-time housekeeper, Lupe, arrived. Since Trish and her family would be moving to a home in the adjacent neighborhood, Lupe offered to help clean Trish's new home and even help her unpack and get organized from the move. Trish graciously accepted Lupe's offer.

Lupe had worked for Jen for over ten years, and she had become a "member of their family." In addition to generously paying for her weekly work, Jen and her husband occasionally gave gifts to Lupe and her husband. They helped them with a car purchase and even with special items such as much-needed orthodontics for both of their children. Five years ago, Lupe wanted to start a cleaning products business to help her family improve their long-term financial security. Jen loaned her the money which Lupe repaid two years later. The business is doing very well, and Lupe's family has a secure future. With Jen and Lupe's help, Trish and her family quickly settled into their new home. Lupe adjusted her schedule with Jen and the other family she worked for to help Trish as much as possible, especially during the first few weeks. With the kids doing well at school and her husband enjoying his new job, Trish was thankful to God for their new home in Smalltown.

Jen and Trish were walking in the park one afternoon, and the discussion turned to the recent Sunday sermon at their church. Their senior pastor was in a series, discussing the biblical truths on several current controversial topics—this past week was on immigration. The central theme of the sermon was that God's plan for immigration, as supported by the Bible, is focused on a government that will affirm the sovereignty of the nation and protect its borders.

Government authorities are called "God's ministers to you for good" and are "an avenger to execute wrath on him who practices evil" (Rom. 13:4–5). This government protection includes securing our borders by whatever means necessary (see Jer. 1–6 and Acts 17:26). The government is also responsible for enforcing all laws including immigration laws (see Rom. 13:1–2). We are a nation of laws and borders—laws to be enforced and borders to be protected.

The message also focused on the compassion of God toward immigrants. Interestingly, the pastor pointed out that the Old Testament Hebrew text makes a distinction between two kinds of immigrants: the "stranger" *(gar* in Hebrew*)* who entered Israel and followed legal procedures to obtain residence as an alien (eventually becoming citizens) and the "foreigner" *(nokri* in Hebrew*)* who refused to assimilate, did not conform to God's laws, and who never became legal citizens. Recognizing we were all immigrants at one time, God commands us to welcome the stranger, "not mistreat him" (Lev. 19:33), and "love him as yourself" (Lev. 19:34). We are called to help the stranger (Deut. 24:14–15), and there was even a "poor tithe" to be given to support in part the stranger (Deut. 14:28–29). In the New Testament, Jesus modeled love and compassion to the stranger in the parables of the Good Samaritan (Luke 10:25–37) and the Samaritan woman at the well (John 4:1–26). The Scripture is very clear that the immigrant who assimilated into culture, respected the laws, and pursued lawful residence and citizenship, was to be welcomed and treated well.

The pastor contrasted the biblical history of the foreigner. When Israel left Egypt, there was a "mixed multitude" (Exod. 12:38), a reference to a group of "foreigners" who accompanied them. This group was not rejected, but if they were going to be a part of Israel, there was an expectation that they would assimilate into Israeli culture and follow Israeli laws (there were ten requirements put on foreigners outlined in the five books of Moses in the Old Testament). Foreigners who assimilated and followed the laws effectively were given the same love and compassion as the strangers. If the foreigner refused to assimilate and adopt Jewish culture or violated the law, they were not welcome and would receive no benefits from living in the land.

Trish praised the message and further offered her opinion that the Bible supports that those in this country illegally should be deported. While Jen also appreciated the message, she did not agree with mass deportation as she believed the compassion Jesus showed the immigrant commands us as Christians to welcome all people into this country. She instead offered amnesty as the solution to the immigration problem and pointed to the example of Lupe and her husband as good people who would benefit from amnesty. Trish was startled to learn for the first time that Lupe was in this country illegally. She could not believe Jen would support a policy like amnesty that effectively protected and rewarded those who had voluntarily broken the law and disregarded the millions of immigrants who gained residency and citizenship by properly following the law.

She expressed her disappointment and displeasure that Jen, as a Christian, knowingly would support illegal activity and continued to do so by retaining an illegal immigrant like Lupe to work for her. Jen quickly defended Lupe and responded that as a Christian, she would never apologize for showing care and compassion to another human.

Trish was clearly agitated and offered a convenient excuse to abruptly end their walk. As she was leaving, she asked Jen to please call Lupe and tell her not to come to her home later that week for her regular cleaning. The next day, when Trish and Jen saw each other at a school function, there was a palpable tension between them. The two close friends were in a conflict that threatened to impact their relationship as well as the lives of their families and others. After a few days of not talking to one another, Jen reached out to Trish, and they agreed to meet.

As Christians who share a fundamentally similar worldview, we are called to "live in peace with each other" (1 Thess. 5:13 NIV). God loves peace, and peace is a part of His character. Since we are made in God's image, He commands us to pursue peace (Ps. 34:14) and promises to bless us when we do (Matt. 5:9). Pursuing a peaceful resolution to any conflict is not only desired and commanded by God, but when successful, the relationship and both individuals will be blessed. However, even though conflict resolution is a desired objective consistent with God's command, only through a thoughtful loving process will the conflict *both* be resolved and the relationship strengthened.

> Preparing our hearts and inviting the Lord to partner with us in the (conflict) resolution is critical.

"Failing to prepare is preparing to fail."[18]

Before resolving any problem of any complexity, especially a conflict involving our closest relationships, we should thoughtfully prepare our hearts. Proverbs 16:1 declares, "The preparations of the heart belong to man, But the answer of the tongue is from the Lord." Remember, conflicts come from the passions that wage war in our hearts.

> God is sovereign; nothing is chaotic to him.

Therefore, preparing our hearts and inviting the Lord to partner with us in the resolution is critical. Our loving Lord is in control of any seemingly chaotic situation. He is sovereign; nothing is chaotic to Him.

In our preparation, it is also important to define and separate the issues. In chapter 1, we examined the definition of conflict. A biblical view of conflict that separates and emphasizes the individuals/participants as opposed to the underlying issue of the conflict creates a pathway to resolution and the preservation of the relationship. Personal issues involve the attitudes and feelings the individuals have toward others as a result of how we have treated one another.[19] Personal issues can generally be resolved by applying the biblical principles of release, confession, loving correction, and forgiveness. Material issues involve substantive matters such as property; money; rights; responsibilities;[20] and, in this time of increasing relative Christian values, biblical truth. By separating the personal and material issues, we create a framework to not only resolve the conflict(s) but also potentially clear up any bitterness or resentments (previously undisclosed personal issues) that have been lingering beneath the surface.

The final step before entering into any conflict resolution discussions with our Christian brother or sister is "to shod [our] feet with the preparation of the gospel of peace" (Eph. 6:15). Paul used this image to illustrate the firm foundation on which Christians are to stand. Remember, the enemy's primary objective is to destroy the relationship. We need to be armed with spiritual weapons to protect both us and our friend as we work together toward a resolution. Properly armed with our hearts prepared and determined to love each other well, we are now positioned to resolve any conflicts.

As Jen and Trish prepared to meet to discuss the issues regarding Lupe, they should select a location that is warm, comfortable, and conducive to a spirit-filled discussion. While either of their homes might be a perfectly suitable setting, they should keep in mind that the goal is not to "win the argument." Love is guiding the discussion; therefore, neither of them should seek a "home field advantage." Often a quiet area of the church or outdoors in a park where there would be little to no distraction is the ideal location. Finally, they should give themselves sufficient time to promote the desired relaxed environment (i.e., do not try to squeeze this discussion in between two other important appointments).

Jen and Trish decided to meet in the foyer of the sanctuary of their church at 10:00 a.m. Very few people, if any, are in that area on a weekday morning, so it was an ideal place to meet. Neither had any appointments on their respective calendars until later in the afternoon, so they allocated plenty of time for their discussion. They opened in prayer, inviting the Holy Spirit to be with them and bless their time together. It is important to recognize that while prayer is how we communicate with God and how we draw closer to Him, prayer also improves our relationships with each other. Research indicates that praying together increases respect and improves communication which are two of the relationship disciplines essential to loving through conflict.[21]

While inviting God into an important discussion through prayer is powerful, so is a simple blessing or affirmation. To affirm something is to confirm its truth and to strengthen it. When we bless another person, we speak truth into his or her life. Following their prayer, Jen and Trish each took the opportunity to affirm each other. Jen shared that she has always considered Trish a sister and valued her faith and wisdom. Trish thanked Jen for her graciousness over the years, especially her help with their recent move to Smalltown. They both shared how much they value their friendship. They were now properly prepared to discuss the substantive issues.

Embedded in the substantive issues underlying any conflict are the interests of the parties involved. Interests refer to the concerns, desires, needs, or other things valued by each person. Love challenges us to "look out not only for [our] own interests, but also for the interest of others" (Phil. 2:4). Even if our desired outcomes may be different by respecting and considering each other's interests in love, we are much more likely to resolve our conflicts. Therefore, as each person shares his or her position and desired outcome on the issue(s), it is extremely helpful to also share his or her interests—the key things they value.

Jen began by explaining the close relationship and love she and her family have developed for Lupe and her family. They have worked so hard to build a quality life in the US. She does not want to see that disrupted, especially for their children who have a real opportunity to go to college and secure a great future for themselves. She does not condone illegal activity but believes the overarching principles of the Bible require Christians to extend hospitality to foreigners (Heb. 13:2) as the Lord watches over them (Ps. 146:9). She wants to extend grace to Lupe and her family whom she believes are not in the category of illegal immigrants that Christians should be concerned with.

Trish shared the problems she personally experienced with illegal immigration when she lived in McAllen, Texas, a city on the Mexico border. She witnessed firsthand a significant increase in crime, loss of jobs, and community division, including in her church. She, too, has compassion for many of these people, but as she studied her Bible for wisdom, she believes it clearly calls for "every soul [to] be subject to the governing authorities…[as] appointed by God…and whoever resists the authority resists the ordinance of God" (Rom. 13:1–2). Her interests are that this country is a safe place for its citizens and for those who are granted temporary legal status (i.e., student or work visas) to achieve their best. She respects Lupe's hard work and appreciates how she and her family have assimilated to American values. She also is pleased to know that Lupe and her family are faithful Christians.

Jen and Trish listened to each other respectfully with care and concern for each other. They were intentionally listening to the emotions behind the spoken words as well as each other's body language and nonverbal actions. Trish was very prepared with notes on the biblical support for her position and thoughtfully articulated them to Jen. Jen was less prepared, but her knowledge of the Gospel and Jesus's compassion for the marginalized poured through in her impassioned comments.

When the emotions and passions occasionally elevated, Jen and Trish were able to reflect on the blessings and affirmations they had shared with each other in the opening. This enabled them to maintain a respectful tone throughout their discussion. They were both committed that love would carry them through this conflict. While Trish clearly had the stronger "technical" biblical position, rather than seeing this as a competitive negotiation in which the goal was for her "to defeat Jen," she remembered Philippians 2:4. As a Christian, she was commanded to look out for Jen's interest.

As Jen reflected on Trish's thoughtful analysis of the issues, she began to appreciate a different perspective on immigration supported by the truth of God's Word. It was not just Trish's persuasive presentation that moved Jen, but how she and her family's experiences living near the border had shaped her position. Her love and respect for her friend gave her confidence they could resolve this conflict.

As the discussion continued, it became clear that Jen and Trish shared the similar interest of compassion for immigrants who may have entered this country illegally but who worked hard to assimilate and respect this country's values and freedoms. Anytime the parties in a conflict resolution can identify a shared interest or point of agreement, they have a pathway to resolve the conflict. Seizing this pathway, Trish asked Jen if Lupe would be open to pursuing legal citizenship. Jen shared that she remembered many years ago Lupe telling her that she had given two thousand dollars to an immigration attorney to evaluate her options. The attorney ended up doing no work and shortly thereafter closed his office taking Lupe's money. Jen remembers how discouraged Lupe was when she shared this experience with her. Trish recalled her husband mentioning to her that a well-respected immigration attorney was in the office suite next to his and that they had lunch a few times and struck up a friendship. Jen agreed to follow up with Lupe on her interest in pursuing legal immigration status, and Trish would talk to her husband about engaging the immigration attorney to possibly help Lupe.

> In a conflict situation, the love commandment requires a Christian to make the other's case their own.

The love inherent in being concerned for the interest of others is the same love in the commandment to "love your neighbor as yourself" (Matt. 22:39). In a conflict situation, a Christian must make the other's case their own. It is a selfless love that may require us to deny ourselves or yield our own interests for the good of our neighbor. When we do, we create a clear path for conflicts to be resolved. We genuinely rejoice in the prosperity of our Christian friends as much or more as we do our own prosperity.

Over the course of the following weeks, Jen spoke with Lupe who was open to learning more about her options but was hesitant to spend any money until she had more information. Thereafter, Trish's husband spoke with his new friend the immigration attorney, whom he learned was a Christian. He reviewed Lupe and her husband's preliminary information, and after meeting with both, he agreed to help her gain legal status and eventual citizenship. He further agreed to do the work at a reduced fee which Lupe and her husband could afford, and agreed to bill her at the end of the engagement (as he wanted to soften their fears from their previous experience with the other attorney). The process would take a year or longer to complete, but his office would provide regular updates. Although one of his associates would take the lead on this, he would personally make himself available to answer any questions. God clearly had His hand on what was happening, and Jen and Trish were confident that this was a solution that would glorify Him.

Months later, Jen and Trish were sharing the story of their relationship challenge with their women's pastor. As they each shared, it was clear that they successfully resolved their conflict through the combination of the thoughtful and planned process as well as their mutual commitment to love each other well throughout that process. Their pastor pointed out one of the important truths from the famous "love" passage in 1 Corinthians 13:5: Love "does not seek its own." She further explained that love is opposed to selfishness. This does not mean that we neglect ourselves, but it means that we do not pursue our own interests at the expense of others or if it will hurt others. Neither Jen nor Trish neglected their own interests; instead, they thoughtfully balanced their own interests with the interest of the other (as well as considering the interests of Lupe and the community/public). Their pastor also reminded them that even the closest friendships like theirs will likely be tested again (see John

16:33). She encouraged them to journal about this experience so as to always remember the process that strengthened their relationship and enabled them to resolve the conflict.

When we approach a conflict in love as Jen and Trish demonstrated, we engage in a cooperative, as opposed to a competitive, process-seeking solutions that benefit everyone involved. As we will examine in chapter 9, we should never compromise the truth of the Bible or God's will. However, when we are aligned in His truth and His will, a cooperative process based in love will strengthen the relationship and often lead to win-win-win solutions. Jen, Trish, Lupe, and their families all benefited from loving through conflict. More importantly, God was glorified. Amen.

Conflict Impasse—Love Preserves the Relationships

The Bridges Church ("Bridges"), a nondenominational, disciple-making church, has experienced tremendous growth over the past five years under the leadership of their senior pastor, Stephen. Two years ago, as part of a church-planting strategy that Pastor Stephen had successfully implemented a decade earlier at a former church, Bridges began launching five "satellite/home" churches in neighboring communities. Each church was hosted by two members of Bridges staff and supported by church volunteers who lived or worked in the respective community. The pastoral staff assigned to each church had the responsibility to help market and grow the church with the financial and logistical support of the Bridges parent church.

North Hills was a low-income neighborhood that was experiencing a revival after the nearby military base was closed several years earlier. There were no major churches in the area, so Pastor Stephen thought this was an ideal area to plant a church to meet the community's needs. The Bridges secured a small vacant industrial space that had some capacity for growth as the temporary home for Bridges—North Hills.

Kevin and Theresa were selected as the Bridges staff members to lead the North Hills church plant. Both were in their early thirties and married with young children. Although they served in different areas at Bridges, they both had been on staff for many years and were friends. Kevin's background was in community outreach, having served in the outreach department of a large church after graduating from Bible college. After Theresa earned her MBA, she spent two years as a missionary in Africa before joining the Bridges team to work on a small-group curriculum. Kevin and Theresa's respective skills and spiritual gifts complemented each other, and God blessed the North Hills church plant with steady growth. After fifteen months with North Hills's strong and growing attendance at their temporary location, the Bridges Elder Board decided to allow North Hills to become an independent church. They identified a vacant church in an ideal location as North Hills's new permanent home.

Pastor Stephen met with Kevin and Theresa to inform them of the plans to transition North Hills to independence. The transition plan called to hire a full-time lead pastor to not only serve in an executive role in running the church but also minister to the needs of the congregation and community. North Hills would continue to livestream Pastor Stephen's weekly message, but the lead pastor would preach a live sermon once a month until the legal control and full transition were complete at the end of one year. The current membership and financial base would support a small initial staff including the management positions of a community life pastor and outreach director. Pastor Stephen asked Kevin and Theresa to each pray about their interest in possibly joining the new North Hills team.

Following the meeting, Theresa was excited to share the news of the North Hills independence plan with her husband and several close friends. As she prayed over this, Theresa believed that God had equipped her for the lead pastor position. While she had no prior experience leading a church, she had a major advantage over other potential candidates in that she had built strong relationships with the North Hills congregation and volunteers. They knew her and liked her. Although neither she nor Kevin had ever preached a sermon, they were on the stage for the opening and closing of every church service, and she had always felt comfortable addressing a large group. In addition, over the past two years, she had been part of the teaching rotation for the main women's Bible study at Bridges, so she felt more than capable of preaching a sermon to a larger audience. Finally, she was confident her MBA and general business knowledge would provide a solid foundation to run the business operations of the church. When Theresa met with her women's small group later that week and asked them to pray for her, she was encouraged that God was about to open an exciting new door for her.

A few days before their scheduled meeting with Pastor Stephen, Kevin and Theresa had lunch following the Sunday service at North Hills. Their respective families had gotten to know each other well through their North Hills leadership, and they had developed a strong working relationship and friendship. Theresa shared that she was very interested in the lead pastor position. Kevin's wife was expecting their third child in a few months, and as he had prayed, he knew that the timing was not right to pursue such a demanding job. Instead, he was very interested in continuing with North Hills in the outreach director position. He enjoyed this work and was energized at the prospect of implementing several creative ideas to effect real change in the community and to help the North Hills congregation grow spiritually. He was excited at Theresa's interest in the lead pastor position and would fully support her. They both left lunch excited at the prospects of continuing to work together and helping transition North Hills to independence.

Accompanying Pastor Stephen at the North Hills transition meeting was the chairman of the Bridges' Elder Board, John, and the executive pastor, Fred. Kevin and Theresa joined the meeting along with their senior volunteer, Jerry, who was also an elder at Bridges. After opening in prayer, Pastor Stephen began the meeting by thanking Kevin and Theresa for their leadership in building such a strong and stable congregation to make this independence transition possible. After reviewing some of the projected financials and business logistics that the board had approved as part of the transition plan, the discussion turned to the key staff positions at North Hills: the lead pastor, community life pastor, and outreach director. Theresa's heart began to race as she sifted through her papers for the copies of the professionally bound executive summary of her qualifications for the lead pastor position that she had prepared. Before she had a chance to speak, Pastor Stephen shared that he had recommended to the board that Kevin be elevated to become the lead pastor and for Theresa to serve as the community life pastor. As Kevin's eyes turned to Theresa, he saw the dejection on her face. He quickly responded with a polite "thank you" to Pastor Stephen for considering him for the lead pastor position but shared that he believed Theresa was more qualified and prepared for the job. Pastor Stephen was surprised by the turn of events and asked to take a short recess.

When the meeting resumed, Pastor Stephen reiterated his thanks to Theresa and Kevin for their work at North Hills. John was passing out copies of the Bridges's bylaws which had a section conspicuously highlighted, stating that "governing and teaching roles in the church are reserved for men." There was a reference that the position is consistent with the "Danvers Statement" from the Council on Biblical Manhood and Womanhood and is supported by 1 Timothy 2:11–15. Pastor Stephen went on to explain that the North Hills lead pastor position was both a governing and teaching role, and since Bridges would have legal control of the church for the first year, unfortunately, Theresa could not be considered for the position. He asked both Kevin and Theresa to reconsider the board's recommendation and that they would reconvene next week for a follow-up meeting. Theresa maintained her composure as she gathered her materials and left the meeting. Kevin attempted to talk to her as they were exiting the building, but she politely told him that she needed to get home to her kids as she wiped tears from her face.

In the days that followed, as Theresa processed her thoughts, she met with several people beginning with her close friend, Tammy, the women's pastor at Bridges. Theresa was surprised when Tammy shared that she was familiar with the statement in Bridges's bylaws as she remembered reading it when she joined the pastoral staff at the church. Tammy explained that doctrinally many Protestant denominations and nondenominational churches like Bridges follow the "complementarian" position that emphasizes that men and women, while equal in value, have complimentary differences. While complementarian churches may differ on specifically which roles women can serve, most, if not all of them, prohibit women from having authority over the whole church. Bridges allowed for women to serve in "supporting" teaching roles consistent with Tammy's position as the women's pastor. The next day, when Theresa met with her small group, many of the women were visibly upset by what they perceived was an outdated and chauvinistic policy. One of the group members, Cindy, who graduated from seminary and who was a teacher at a Christian high school, explained the egalitarian doctrine which supports perfect equality between men and women. This doctrine states that all church positions are open to men and women alike and is supported by Galatians 3:28 and Judges 4–5. The egalitarian doctrine is fully summarized in the Christians for Biblical Equality group statement called Men, Women, and Biblical Equality. Another woman in the group, a civil rights attorney, shared that a woman in a church in the Midwest had successfully sued the church to get equal job treatment although she did not recall the specific facts of that case. As tensions rose, others in the group expressed their frustration and began talking about possibly boycotting church services or even picketing. Tammy, who was also in the group, quickly de-escalated the situation and cautioned the women to allow Theresa to continue to process the issues before considering taking any action.

As Theresa left the group, she was confused and emotionally drained. She had genuinely felt that God had prepared her for the North Hills lead pastor position, but at what cost? Did God want her to fight Bridges's policy against women serving in governing positions? Theresa was in the middle of a conflict. She needed God's wisdom and His love to help guide her.

As discussed in chapter 3, when we know God (Father, Son, and Holy Spirit), our love for Him can overflow into our relationships with others. Love comes from God who personifies the attribute. This attribute of God shows that it is part of His nature to give of Himself in order to bring about blessing or good for others. God's love means that God eternally gives of Himself to others. The eternal love between the Father, the Son, and the Holy Spirit is our example of how each person of the Trinity seeks to bring joy and happiness to the other two.

The two love commandments in Matthew 22:37–39 describe both our vertical relationship with God and the horizontal relationship with others. Neither portray a love that is an emotion but describe love as an action. Love for one's neighbor means acting toward others with their good, their well-being, and their fulfillment as the primary motivation and goal of our deeds.[22] This love is constant and does not seek to value the merit of the other person or the merit of their position (assuming it is supported by the truth of God's Word and His will). This commandment is referenced by Paul in Romans 13:9 as "the summing up of all the commandments," in Galatians 5:14 as "the fulfillment of the whole law," and in James 2:8 as "fulfilling the royal law according to scripture."[23] This supports Jesus's teaching on love which is the fundamental ground upon which the New Testament church is built.

Theresa continued to pray for discernment. She and Kevin had their regular weekly meeting to prepare for the Sunday service at North Hills. It was the first time they had seen each other or spoken since the meeting with Pastor Stephen. Kevin reiterated to Theresa that despite Pastor Stephen's recommendation, he had no interest in the lead pastor position. He further reassured her that he valued their friendship and how much he enjoyed serving together over the past fifteen months. While he did not offer any commentary on the church's position on women serving in governing roles and after they closed their meeting in prayer, he reaffirmed his support for her and reminded her that "all things work together for good to those who love God, to those who are the called according to His purpose" (Rom. 8:28). She thanked him and left for Bridges to pick up some materials for the weekend. She ran into Tammy who offered her support and continued prayers. Tammy shared how much the members of their Life Group respected her as a godly woman, and she was confident that whatever Theresa decided to do, the group would support her.

Pastor Stephen's message on Sunday was on the "Kingdom of God." As illustrated in John 3, the kingdom of God is often misunderstood by Christians as it was by Nicodemus, a respected teacher in Israel. Pastor Stephen explained that Jesus helped Nicodemus understand that the kingdom of God is here and now. In Matthew 6:33, Jesus commands us to "seek first the kingdom of God and His righteousness." The kingdom of God is God in action. It is what God is doing where we are. When we seek the kingdom of God, we are seeking more and more to allow God to be present in everything that we are and everything that we do, and we allow Him to act and overrule and guide and help us become what He intended us to be.[24] Through the love of Christ, we are bearers of the kingdom of God. The message penetrated Theresa's heart as she continued to seek discernment from God.

Webster's Dictionary defines impasse as a situation offering no escape, as a difficulty without solution, an argument where no agreement is possible, etc.[25]

Not all conflicts or disagreements will be resolved. From the beginning of time, Christians have disagreed on numerous issues including "minor" theological doctrines such as infant baptism and transubstantiation.[26] In such situations, both parties honestly believed they were objectively following the truth of God's Word. As discussed in chapter 1, because we are made in God's image and each of us is wonderfully unique, we will see things differently. Every issue or position does not necessarily have a right or wrong answer, including from God's perspective.

> Every issue or position does not necessarily have a right or wrong answer, including from God's perspective.

The secular definition of an impasse suggests that there is "no escape" or "no agreement is possible." However, Christians know that God is faithful, and He can make "a way of escape" (1 Cor. 10:13) from any situation. The path he provides to move us through an impasse is love. When we choose to love, while the substance of the disagreement or conflict may not be resolved, we maintain the integrity and strength of our relationships. We also bring glory to God and allow His blessings to flow not only to the parties in the conflict but also to the kingdom of God. We live out the Lord's Prayer as Jesus gave us in Matthew 6:10: "Your kingdom come. Your will be done, On earth as it is in heaven." When Christians are at an impasse we have a solution, let God's love freely flow through us. He will make a way.

Theresa had follow-up discussions with both Tammy and Kevin as she prepared for Wednesday's meeting with Pastor Stephen and the transition team. She did some independent research on the complementarian and egalitarian doctrines but more importantly, she continued to pray for discernment. When she awoke on Wednesday morning, she felt a strong peace and clarity that God was directing her steps. She fitted herself in the armor of God and left for the Bridges's offices.

After opening the meeting in prayer, Pastor Stephen once again praised Theresa and Kevin for their work at North Hills over the past fifteen months. He confirmed the church's strong desire that they both continue with North Hills through the independence succession plan and asked each of them if they had an opportunity to prayerfully consider the recommendation he had presented at last week's meeting. Infused with the Holy Spirit, Theresa took the initiative to respond first. She began by affirming Pastor Stephen and the Elder Board for their vision to grow the church to the benefit of the North Hills community. She also thanked him for entrusting her and Kevin to shepherd the neighborhood church which had enabled her to experience significant personal spiritual growth. She honestly confessed her disappointment at the Bridges's position prohibiting women from serving in governing or teaching positions. Without going into too much technical detail, she summarized why she believed the egalitarian position is not only supported by the Bible but, in her opinion, is consistent with Bridges's mission to make disciples and serve the community. The fact that over half of the Bridges staff and congregation are women suggests that Bridges's bylaws may be outdated and, at a minimum, require a thoughtful review. Her interest was seeing that God use her gifts, and she believed she was qualified and prepared for the lead pastor position at North Hills. She paused for a second, gathered herself, and continued. However, as she prayed over the past week, God revealed to her that pursuing her own interest might be in opposition to the church's interests (both Bridges and North Hills). If she was to passionately advocate for a woman to serve as the lead pastor, it would likely create a division in the congregation. It would certainly impact the North Hills transition, especially among the volunteers and members with whom Theresa has built close relationships. The doctrinal disagreement might eventually be resolved but such a resolution would likely cause damage to the church and, in doing so, would not glorify God. She concluded her remarks by saying that she would be honored to accept the position as the community life pastor at North Hills. Kevin, who was unaware of Theresa's decision prior to these remarks, smiled at her as he outwardly declared his interest in the outreach director position at North Hills.

Pastor Stephen turned to John and Fred and, with an acknowledging nod, heartily accepted Theresa's and Kevin's new leadership roles at North Hills. He went on to express his appreciation to Theresa for her faithfulness and the way she prayerfully processed the issues. She thanked him and took the opportunity to share a few final thoughts on her deep love for the church. She had worshiped at Bridges for almost ten years and had met her husband at Bridges, and they were married at the church. Her children were dedicated and baptized at the church. When she joined the staff, she began to experience the church from a whole new perspective—Bridges was more than just a church; it was a community of people who were making an impact on the world. She loved Bridges, the staff, the congregation, and the community. This love helped her realize that unity was more important than her being right or getting what she wanted. While several women in the church were praying for her to "stand up for women's rights," she knew that doing so would be playing into the enemy's strategy to divide the church. She trusts God will continue to develop her and that if it is in His will, there will be a future opportunity for her to be a lead pastor. She joked that perhaps she will take over for Pastor Stephen when he retires! The tension that was in the air when the meeting started was replaced by joyful laughter from everyone in the room. God had a huge smile on His face. As the meeting concluded, they prayed, thanking God and asking for His favor on the North Hills transition plan.

It took less than six weeks, but Pastor Stephen secured Pastor Raymond as the North Hills lead pastor. It was an answer to prayer as Pastor Raymond had the perfect combination of childhood ties to the community and outreach experience, and he had several years' experience in leading a small church in another state. Theresa and Kevin warmly welcomed him, and under the leadership of the three, North Hills immediately took off. Within a few months, Pastor Raymond added a Wednesday night service and invited Theresa to preach once a month so she could gain additional experience. Later in the year as part of a comprehensive review of Bridges's governance, mission statement, and bylaws, Pastor Stephen invited Theresa to be part of a subcommittee to study and evaluate the church's position on women in governance and teaching roles. At the end of the year, North Hills officially became an independent church. Its congregation had grown, and it was making a tangible impact on the community. Bridges was able to begin transitioning two other church plants to independence, and one was being led by a woman pastor.

In many conflicts, the substantive issue(s) may not allow for a natural resolution or even a compromise solution. Accordingly, the parties may be at an impasse. If the flesh or pursuit of self-interest dominate either of the parties' thinking, relationships will likely be damaged or destroyed. When Christians instead seek to imitate God and walk in His love, they humbly turn the focus away from themselves and look to the greater good.

> When Christians seek to imitate God and walk in His love, they humbly turn the focus away from themselves and look to the greater good.

Theresa, Kevin, Tammy, and many others loved well during this conflict. As a result, the North Hills transition exceeded expectations, the church grew, and the community was blessed. Pastor Stephen and the Elder Board responded in love with more church plants, successful implementation of independent transitions, and proactively reviewed and modified the Bridges's doctrinal position on women resulting in a woman leading a new church. Through everyone's love in action, relationships were preserved, and God was glorified.

Relationships Redefined to Last— Loving with Boundaries

Emily arrived home at 5:30 p.m. after a grueling day at work. The law firm where she worked as a paralegal was in the middle of a big case and over the past few weeks, the work was so demanding, she barely had time to take a thirty-minute lunch break. However, she always perked up when she walked through the front door at home to her two-year-old son, J. J. When Emily had returned to work following her maternity leave, she had hoped to be able to work from home so she could care for J. J. as she did for her other two children: fourteen-year-old Laney and thirteen-year-old Will. Unfortunately, the job demands would not allow for that, so they hired a full-time nanny/housekeeper, Josephine, to care for him. J. J. was an unexpected addition to their family at age thirty-seven as Emily and her husband, Rick, had not planned to have any more children. J. J. was a blessing, but managing a full-time job while caring for three children, including two teenagers, was taking its toll.

Emily's normal weekday evening routine was to play with J. J. for thirty minutes then put him down for a short nap before preparing dinner. Rick usually got home at 6:30 p.m. from his job as an operations manager at a logistics company. On his way home, he occasionally picked up Laney and Will from their respective school activity, church group, or athletic practice, but sometimes they rode their bikes home or got a ride home from another family. Emily insisted on family dinner at 7:00 p.m., a tradition she grew up with within her own family.

After dinner, Emily sorted through the mail which she dreaded as it contained the usual combination of junk mail and bills. On this day she received the final bill from Rick's knee surgery (he hurt himself golfing six months earlier) as well as the quarterly invoices from Laney's and Will's orthodontist. When Rick had pursued an entrepreneurial venture many years earlier, Emily was put in charge of the bookkeeping by default because of her college accounting degree. At that time, she also took over managing the family finances. Since she returned to work, their financial situation had worsened. Their combined net take-home pay barely covered their regular monthly expenses, and when unexpected periodic expenses hit like Rick's medical bills, she would have to dip into their savings. She had attempted on numerous occasions to sit down with Rick to explain their financial situation; however, Rick would get very defensive, and it would inevitably create tension in the home. When he hurt his knee, playing golf, and she suggested he give up his golf club membership as it was an "unnecessary expense, and he would not be able to use it for a while," it turned into one of the biggest arguments of their marriage. While J. J. was a huge joy in her life, he brought a whole new set of expenses, most notably Josephine. To manage everything, Emily reduced both her and Rick's contributions to their retirement accounts and the children's college savings accounts. This helped, but there was significant financial pressure. And sadly she did not feel comfortable discussing it with her husband.

On Friday nights, Emily had a break from helping the kids with their homework. She had planned to take a relaxing bubble bath, but J. J. was restless. So she asked Rick if he could watch him for an hour. He said he could not as he needed to clean his golf clubs as he reminded her that he had a member golf tournament at his club this weekend. This would be his first opportunity to play since he was cleared by his doctor last week. When she replied that he had never informed her that he would be golfing all weekend, he snapped back that he had told her, and she conveniently forgot since she hates golf.

Rather than engaging further, she decided to put J. J. in his stroller and take a walk through the neighborhood. On the walk, she could not help but notice happy couples holding hands and young parents playing with their kids. She was uneasy with the negative thoughts rolling through her mind. She found a park bench, closed her eyes for a few minutes, and prayed for God to calm her heart.

Weekends were dominated by Laney's soccer and Will's lacrosse games. For years, it was "divide and conquer," as usually Emily would accompany Laney to her games and Rick would take Will to his. J. J. added a new wrinkle as Emily tried hard to keep him on a consistent eating and napping schedule. With Rick golfing all weekend, Emily knew her hands would be full. She managed to get Laney and Will to their respective fields on time. Will had an all-day tournament so that made it easier for her to take J. J. home at lunchtime for a nap. During his nap, she reviewed and updated the grocery shopping list (she always did the weekly shopping on Sunday afternoons). After Laney's game finished, they went to watch Will play but had to leave early as Laney had worship band practice at church. J. J. was taking his afternoon nap when Rick called after his golf round to tell Emily that he was going to have dinner with a few friends, and he would be home later. She reminded him that he was supposed to pick up Will from his tournament. He said he could not and asked her to "figure out something." She woke J. J. from his nap a few minutes early and picked up Will from his tournament and then Laney from church. The kids helped cook dinner, and then after playing with J. J., Emily put him down for bed. She spent the rest of the evening organizing their tax file as she had promised their accountant, and she would drop it off at his office on Monday. When Rick came home at 9:30 p.m., Emily was already asleep following an exhausting day.

Since Will's first tournament game on Sunday was not until 11:00 a.m., they decided to go to church at 9:00 a.m. Rick would not be joining them as he teed off at 9:30 a.m., but he dropped Laney off at church for her preservice thworship practice. Emily cleaned up the breakfast dishes, and she, Will, and J. J. left for church. Emily loved watching Laney play piano and sing with the junior high worship group and the staggered church start times then allowed her and Will to attend the main service in the sanctuary. Church was always one hour of solitude and peace that Emily could count on every week. The message on spiritual leadership was powerful but left her further frustrated with Rick as he regularly chose golf or another activity over church. When they returned home in the late afternoon following Will's tournament, the kids watched J. J. as Emily did the weekly grocery shopping. Rick called as she was leaving the store. He and his partner had won the tournament and were celebrating. He hoped to be home in time for dinner, but he would let her know if he was running late. She congratulated him and reminded him that they had Life Group at 7:00 p.m. He said he would definitely be home by then. At 6:45 p.m., Rick texted and said he would not be home until later, so Emily went to Life Group alone. When she returned home at 8:30 p.m., she put J. J. down to bed and checked on Laney and Will who were finishing up their homework. It was 9:30 p.m. when Rick, who had celebrated a little too much, left his car at the golf club and took an UBER home. The house was quiet as everyone was fast asleep—the weekend was officially over.

Monday mornings were especially chaotic getting ready for work, Laney and Will preparing for school, and Emily awaiting Josephine's arrival. This morning was complicated by the fact that Emily had to drop Rick off at his club to retrieve his car. On the drive there, he shared golf story after golf story about his tournament victory. By the time they got to the club, she never had an opportunity to share about the family's weekend including the sermon message. Emily arrived at work a few minutes late. She had lunch scheduled with her friend Rachel who worked at the building next door. She looked forward to a midday break from another busy morning at work.

Emily ordered a small salad for her lunch as she was self-conscious about her body after Rick's recent comments about her "not having lost enough weight" following J. J.' s birth two years ago. As Emily shared about the recent busy weekend, Rachel was quick to offer her criticism of Rick. This was fueled in part by some of the similar problems she was having in her own marriage. The lunch conversation was dominated by their respective husband's shortcomings and the frustration each was experiencing in believing it would never improve. Emily returned to work even more dejected than when she had started her day. She was making dinner when Laney and Will called asking where Dad was as he was supposed to pick them up from their practice fifteen minutes earlier. Rick walked in moments later, and when she reminded him that he was supposed to pick them up, he angrily replied that she never reminded him this morning. He muttered a rude comment, then left abruptly and went to school to get them. She kept the food warm for them but did not join them for dinner as she tended to J. J. for the rest of the night until his bedtime as Rick watched Monday Night Football. Before she went to bed, she prayed for God to soften her heart which she felt was growing harder every day.

The next day, Rick left early for work as he had a scheduled meeting with his boss to discuss his interest in a new position in the company. While Rick did not have many details about the job, he knew he was qualified for the position and that it paid substantially more than his current salary. Emily prayed and anxiously awaited Rick's update on the meeting. When she finally connected with him later in the morning, he said that he was offered the position which had many attractive qualities, but he was not interested in pursuing it as he would have to occasionally work on Saturdays and that would interfere with his golf schedule and family time. He had to get back to work and said he would share more when he got home.

After dinner, Emily approached Rick to discuss his work meeting in more detail. He did not open up much except to say that he was not interested in working on Saturdays.

When she asked how often he would need to work on Saturdays, he replied, "Maybe once a month."

When she tried to discuss with him that the considerable salary increase would really help their financial situation, he said it would not be worth it to miss golf and the kids' activities. When she reminded him that he had missed the kids' games this past weekend for his golf tournament and two weeks before that when he went with some friends to a football game, he quickly defended himself that he worked hard and was entitled to personal time.

Emily's frustration had reached a peak, and she erupted, calling him selfish. She recanted the history of his failed entrepreneurial venture and that he was unmotivated and lazy to pursue job opportunities to help his family. She pressed on about his lack of attention to the family and his continual criticism of her and her appearance. He yelled back with several unflattering comments about her. His voice was loud enough that both Laney and Will rushed into the room to see what was going on. Rick grabbed his car keys and left. Emily assured the kids that everything was fine, and she sent them back to their rooms to finish their homework. She checked on J. J. who thankfully had slept through the yelling. She sat at the edge of her bed and cried. She was in a conflict, and she did not know how or if it could ever be resolved. She needed God but did not even know what to pray for. She was in distress.

Often our longest and most committed relationships are the most challenging. The familiarity between two people who have been in a lengthy relationship creates a set of expectations of grace and forgiveness that actually can create relationship conflict. Marriage, in many ways, is the most complex of all relationships. The fact that "[two] shall become one flesh" (Gen. 2:24) creates an inherent challenge: we are to give up our separation and become one while at the same time retaining our individual personhood. Emily is experiencing pain as she operates in this state of confusion. She loves Rick and desires to selflessly care for him and serve his interests. However, in doing so, she has allowed Rick to take advantage of her; abdicate his responsibilities in the relationship; and, at times, disregard her feelings. Over some time, she has built up resentments that have spun her out of control and resulted in the outburst and argument. Fortunately, "love covers all sins" (Prov. 10:12), and through her love of God and her love for Rick, God can make a way for Emily to redefine and strengthen her marriage.

All successful relationships, including our relationships with God and Christ, are based on freedom. In their hallmark book *Boundaries* by Dr. Henry Cloud and Dr. John Townsend, they counter one of the myths of boundaries—that boundaries are not loving.[27] They do so by demonstrating that the goal of boundaries is love coming out of freedom.[28] Boundaries allow us to be in control of ourselves and, in doing so, free us to serve others well. When we are in control, we can give and sacrifice for loved ones in a helpful way instead of giving in to destructive behavior and self-centeredness.[29] To follow Philippians 2:4 and "look out not only for [our] own interests but also for the interest of others" must be done out of freedom, not boundaryless compliance.

Relationship boundaries, like physical boundaries, help us to understand what we are responsible for and what the other person is responsible for. In a marriage, there are many individual responsibilities delegated to each spouse as well as many shared responsibilities. When these are not properly communicated, at a minimum, it leads to confusion or, in many cases, a disproportionate share of responsibility assumed by one party. God demonstrated relationship boundaries in His relationship with the other members of the Trinity. The Father, the Son, and the Spirit are one, but at the same time, they are distinct persons with their own boundaries. Each one has His own personhood and responsibilities, as well as a connection with and love for one another (John 17:24). With these boundaries in place, the Trinity operates in perfect love for each other and the world. The same can be true for us when we set healthy boundaries and take control of what is our responsibility. When we take full responsibility for ourselves, we can love others well.

Establishing boundaries involves setting limits. However, it is often misunderstood that setting limits on others is equivalent to trying to change them or the way they behave. We do not have that capability. God does not set limits on people to make them behave properly. He does set standards and gives man free will, and if they misbehave, He separates Himself from them. Over time, they learn to appreciate His love and that His standards are loving. As they appreciate His standards and resume operating within them, their relationship with God is strengthened. Limits have the benefit of providing us with an internal structure to maintain self-control. They provide a foundation for us to separate ourselves from people who hurt us or act destructively. In Matthew 18:15–17, Jesus illustrates the process of loving correction to a sinner and permits separation until such time as they repent, submit, and reconcile back to the church or us. Separation in those situations is not being unloving. Separating ourselves protects love because we are taking a stand against things that destroy love.[30]

Because God designed us to be in a relationship with each other (see chapter 3), boundaries are a necessary tool to help us define these relationships. Boundaries help us love well in our relationships. However, as explained in *Boundaries*, the "Law of Exposure" requires that boundaries need to be made visible to others and communicated to them in relationship.[31] Our boundary problems are often a result of our relational fears such as fears of guilt, not being liked, loss of love, loss of connection, loss of approval, and not being known.[32] These are all failures in love. God's plan for us and commandments to us are that we learn to love and love well.[33] These fears cause us to create secret boundaries which result in us withdrawing passively and quietly instead of communicating honestly with those we love.[34] As a result, we build up resentments, and we privately endure the pain of someone else's irresponsibility. Instead of telling them how their behavior affects other loved ones and us, we deprive them of information that would be helpful to their soul.[35] By not setting and expressing healthy boundaries, we are unloving. Boundaries are not self-centered or selfish, they show our concern and love for others. Boundaries actually increase our ability to love others well.

> Boundaries actually increase our ability to love others well.

When Emily awoke on Monday morning, Rick, who had slept on the couch downstairs, had already left for work. There was a note on the bathroom counter that read:

> Although I am selfish and neglectful, tell
> Laney and Will that I will pick them up from
> practice at 6:00 p.m.

Selfish and *neglectful* were words she had used in their argument. She checked on J. J. who was still sleeping. As she read her morning devotional and prayed, God was encouraging her that she needed to talk to a trusted Christian friend to help her process everything. She typed an email to her friend Beth, requesting time to talk on the phone or meet. Beth volunteered at their church with the junior worship group, and Emily had gotten to know her well since Laney had first joined the group three years ago. Beth and her husband, Jim, an elder in the church, had recently become empty nesters when their youngest son left for college a few months ago. She was a godly woman who was easy to talk to and was comforting to her throughout her unexpected pregnancy and the birth of J. J. When Emily arrived at work, Beth had already replied to her email that she was available to meet or talk at 2:00 p.m. Emily asked her boss if she could take a late lunch. He could see that something was troubling her, so he graciously gave her the afternoon off.

Emily met Beth at the church. As Emily shared the challenges she was facing at home and her frustrations with Rick, Beth attentively listened. After Emily finished, they talked about how Emily felt when Rick disrespected her or when he neglected his responsibilities. Beth also probed Emily about what she desired by way of change. In order to establish healthy boundaries, it is critical to communicate our feelings and desires thoughtfully and lovingly. Beth, who had experienced similar challenges with her husband in their twenty-five years of marriage, gave Emily some wisdom regarding boundaries. She also offered some practical suggestions of boundaries Emily could implement that would not only address her feelings of fear and loneliness but also would help Rick grow and develop to be the man that God called him to be. As they closed in prayer, they agreed to talk regularly, and Beth offered for Rick to meet with Jim who mentors other men.

On her way home, Emily arranged for a friend to pick up Laney and Will from their practices and feed them dinner. She would pick them up from her house at 8:00 p.m. She also dropped J. J. off with her sister who loved watching her favorite nephew. She and Rick would be able to be home alone for a few hours this evening, so she began to pray and prepare for their discussion. As she read through some of the Bible verses Beth gave her and processed some of the suggestions they had discussed, she prayed for God's love to flow through her to Rick and for his heart to be opened to receive it.

When preparing for a discussion on relationship boundaries, it is important to approach it similar to any conflict resolution. You should be mindful to

- imitate God's love through humility, mercy, forgiveness, and loving correction;
- communicate well with honesty, openness, transparency, sensitivity, trust, and respect; and
- prepare for a spiritual attack and equip yourself with the armor of God for successful resistance.

In addition, it is essential to remember that conflicts represent an opportunity to glorify God. Emily had food delivered from Rick's favorite restaurant as she prepared her heart for his arrival.

Rick sensed something was amiss when he walked in the front door to complete silence. He was concerned at first but quickly noticed the dinner table set for two. Moments later, Emily came walking downstairs in his favorite dress; she looked beautiful. She took his hand, and they sat on the couch. She began by praying which included an apology for the hurtful comments she made last night, and she asked for his forgiveness. Before he even had a chance to respond, she took time to affirm him for his numerous wonderful qualities—his patience with the kids, his love for her family as demonstrated when her mother passed away, and his support for her when she had breast cancer five years earlier. He smiled, thanked her, and apologized for any harsh words he may have said during their argument. Any tension that may have existed ten minutes earlier before he arrived home had dissipated. She continued with confidence as she expressed her feelings of financial fear, loneliness, and disrespect. At first, Rick responded defensively; however, Emily patiently let him complete his thoughts before she explained that *she* needed to begin to take responsibility and control for these feelings. She shared her desire to grow intimacy in their relationship, co-parent well, build financial security, and honor God in everything they do. Although she never used the word boundaries, she then proceeded to outline a few specific "changes" she needed to implement to address these fears and desires:

1. Family dinners would start at 7:00 p.m. sharp. If he was not home by then, he would need to either get dinner on his own or eat leftovers.
2. He would watch J. J. for at least thirty minutes each weeknight to give her an opportunity to relax and care for herself.
3. She had been lax in her spiritual discipline. She was recommitting herself to daily prayer, reading her Bible, Life Group, church worship, and volunteer work. She would love for them to do many of these together including praying in the morning, something they regularly did when they were first married.
4. She was installing a weekly family calendar that would be posted on the refrigerator. It would list out the kids' activities and any other scheduled events to avoid any miscommunications and assign responsibility when appropriate.

Emily presented these items with a combination of boldness and softness that disarmed the normal reactionary response from Rick. He felt the emotion as she expressed her feelings and desires. Although he pushed hard for his own thirty minutes of evening relax time as the discussion concluded, he was otherwise agreeable to these items.

They enjoyed dinner together. It had been a very long time since they were alone in their own home for a meal. As they finished, Emily asked Rick if they could sit down to discuss one more important item. She now felt confident she could address the biggest and most important issue: their finances. She handed him a couple of financial reports she had prepared. As he perused them, he asked why she had never shown them to him before. Rather than get defensive by saying she had tried on many occasions to discuss the subject with him; instead, she apologized and accepted responsibility for not being as open and transparent about the family finances as she should have been.

She walked him through the reports that showed that they were running at an operating deficit of approximately $10,000/year over the past two years. In addition, if they wanted to meet their long-term retirement and college savings goals, they should have contributed an additional $12,000/year to those accounts. Before sharing the key boundary she wanted to implement, she needed to define the boundary problem and origin of the conflict. This is often a critical step in presenting a boundary and providing a foundational explanation for easier boundary acceptance. They proceeded to have a healthy discussion about Rick's failed business venture. Emily shared that she never regretted them taking a chance on entrepreneurial success, and she did not blame him at all for the fact it did not work out. He acknowledged that the experience left him fearful of exploring any new opportunities or even opportunities for advancement in his current job. When he also mentioned being cut from his high school football team, it revealed that there may be deeper issues of fear he had never shared before. She encouraged him by affirming his business skills, work ethic, and talent. She was now ready to present the financial boundary.

She explained that the $10,000 annual deficit was not sustainable. There were two alternatives: (1) he needed to pursue the promotion he was offered, or (2) he needed to resign his golf club membership (she had provided him a schedule showing that the total cost of the membership last year was $9,450). She told him that if he took the promotion, she would handle whatever was needed with the kids on Saturdays.

He responded for the first time, saying the new position may allow for him to work a longer day during the week by coming in early or staying late. She assured him that they could make adjustments as needed, including getting Laney and Will rides home from their activities. She concluded by saying that she knows how much he enjoys golf, and she wants him to have things that bring him joy. However, if they do not address this issue, the family will be in an even more challenging situation in a few years. They even laughed together when she reminded him that, in three years, J. J. would be in kindergarten and, in four years, Laney would be going off to college and Will would be a senior in high school. They embraced and closed in prayer.

The next evening, Rick left work a little early to pick up Laney from her band practice at church. Beth's husband, Jim, happened to be there as they had a church function that evening. As they were catching up on life, Rick shared about his recent "boundary" discussion with Emily and how he struggled with deciding whether to accept the job promotion. Jim shared his own experience with boundaries in his marriage and how much the command of Ephesians 5:25 has helped him: "Husbands love your wives, just as Christ also loved the church and gave Himself for her."

He went on to explain that Jesus's sacrifice tells husbands what it means to love. We love by choice, not by feeling. Biblical love focuses on the need of the person being loved, not necessarily on the emotions or wants of the loving one.[36] It is righteously and passionately pursuing the well-being of the other, even if it comes at personal cost or sacrifice. Jim's experience is that wise and loving husbands will accept boundaries and act responsibly toward them.[37] Those who are controlling and self-centered will react angrily.[38] Jim encouraged Rick to pray for Emily. He explained that if you want to see God enrich your marriage, then pray for your wife. When a wife knows that her husband is praying for her, it makes her feel loved and protected.[39] Rick thanked Jim for his time—this was clearly wisdom from a man who put Jesus in the center of his marriage. Over the following few weeks, Emily and Rick had several more discussions as the boundaries/changes were implemented. Rick began meeting regularly with Jim who became a trusted spiritual mentor.

Rick accepted the promotion which included a $25,000/year annual raise. He arranged to start his workday thirty minutes early so that he would be home in time for family dinners. They began attending Saturday night church service as a family so that on the few occasions when Rick had to work on a Saturday, they would have all of Sunday for other family activities. Rick even encouraged Emily to take golf lessons so they would have a fun activity to share together.

The posted family calendar was a little confusing at first and led to several disagreements, but all issues were eventually resolved.

Over time, Rick learned to respect the boundaries established by Emily. When we respect other's boundaries, they will respect ours. In doing so, we practice the Golden Rule (Matt. 7:12) and love each other well. If we love and respect people who tell us no, they will love and respect our no.[40] Godly love flows not only when we say yes to each other but also when we say no. Emily and Rick continued to have occasional conflicts between each other and with their children—conflicts are unavoidable. They successfully used boundaries and other spiritual tools to love each other well through the conflict, and as a result, they grew closer as a family. Christians with mature boundaries exhibit control in their lives. Control allows them to love their neighbor well, especially in times of conflict.

> Christians with mature boundaries exhibit control in their lives. Control allows them to love their neighbor well, especially in times of conflict.

CHAPTER 9

Forgiveness and Reconciliation— Unifying Love through Conflict

Andrew left the camping store to pick up a few items for next weekend's Mountain View Church Men's Retreat at Shady Woods. As he was driving home, he began to reflect on last year's retreat and the experience he had with his thirteen-year-old son, Tommy, and his then close friend, Jeff Rhodes, and his son, Sam. So much had changed over the past year that he had not spoken to Jeff in almost nine months. They had been such good friends, and their respective families were close as well until the issue of Sam's sexual identity not only drove a wedge between them but also caused division in their church and community.

Andrew had recently learned that in addition to a group of approximately one hundred men from Mountain View Church, there would be a group of men from nearby Bethany Church, coming to Shady Woods for their men's retreat the same weekend. In fact, the two churches would be doing a couple of activities together including the big worship event on the final night of the retreat. Andrew knew from a common friend that Jeff and his family now attended Bethany after leaving Mountain View last fall. He wondered if Jeff would be at the retreat. If so, when they met what would they say to one another? He began to replay the events of last summer in his mind as God began working on his heart.

Last year, when they arrived at Shady Woods following the two-hour drive, Jeff told Andrew he had changed the room assignment and had requested a two-man cabin as he and Sam needed to spend some time together over the weekend. He arranged for Andrew and Tommy to have their own cabin which worked out fine. Throughout the weekend, Andrew noticed that Sam, who was normally pretty spirited and engaged, was instead detached. He was a good athlete and chose not to participate in the big team competition. Tommy had, even on a few occasions, reached out to Sam to encourage him to join one of the special activities organized for the teenagers, but he declined. Andrew remembered Jeff telling him that Sam was not feeling well, so he did not probe any further. The weekend was otherwise very enjoyable with great speakers, discussions, and fun activities. On the ride home, Sam did not speak a word, and Andrew even sensed some tension between Jeff and Sam. He knew something was amiss, and he would follow up with his friend at a more appropriate time.

A few days following the retreat, Andrew and Jeff met for lunch. It was then that Jeff disclosed that over the previous few months that he and his wife, Sarah, had begun noticing some behavioral changes in Sam. He was not only withdrawn but except tennis, in which he was an excellent player for his age, his interests had totally changed. They found several women's fashion magazines in his room, and he had boxed up most of his favorite toys and games in his closet. One afternoon, Sarah came home early from work and found Sam in his older sister's room with makeup on and trying on a few of her dresses. That evening, Sam shared with them his desire to be a girl.

Andrew remembered the anguish on Jeff's face as he continued to share about a recent meeting they had with a friend who was a child psychiatrist as they navigated unchartered territory. They intended to keep this matter private for now, and with the exception of a few family members, no one yet knew of the issue. Jeff further shared that he more or less made Sam attend the men's retreat in hopes that the male camaraderie would help him "snap out" of what he believed was a confused phase. However, it only seemed to make things worse as their discussions throughout the weekend were unproductive and culminated in a big argument when they returned home. Sarah and Jeff had decided to seek guidance from the church. Since Andrew was well connected to both the men's pastor and senior pastor at Mountain View, they asked for his assistance in scheduling a meeting. Andrew agreed to help, and they prayed together as they finished their lunch.

As the world's religious landscape continues to change rapidly, the Christian church has been at the center of a movement that has radically altered the church model. In response to the postmodern culture, the emphasis has shifted from the teaching of Scripture to a "social justice" gospel designed to be more "seeker-sensitive." As a result, the Bible's core teaching of repentance and forgiveness of sins has been replaced by doctrines such as universalism, resulting in a gradual deviation from the authority of Scripture. Instead of seeking the Bible as the sole authority for answers on critical issues, the church, under pressure from a developing "Christian left" faction, has begun to be influenced by the state and mainstream media. This has increased confusion for Christians on many important issues including transgenderism.

Transgenderism, seeing one's self as opposite of the individual's sex at birth, is one of several current cultural battles moving for gender neutrality, a desire to discard the male-female distinction. Advocates of gender neutrality have attempted to change the definition of gender from a classification based on biological sex to a classification based on one's internal sense of themselves as being either male, female, or other, regardless of biology. The Bible provides critical guidance on the issue from its very beginning in Genesis 1:27, "So God created man in His own image; in the image of God He created him; male and female He created them."

Foundational to God's plan for the world was the core value of two distinct sexes for a sexual union to perpetuate mankind. This "twoness" of male and female becomes the basis for a heterosexual monogamous relationship that clearly creates the biblical standard for sexual and relational identity. An identity that opposes practices such as polygamy, serial divorce and remarriage, homosexuality, and any transgender relationships.

Although Jesus in the New Testament Gospels never specifically mentioned transgenders, He did support the Mosaic Law. He declared in Matthew 5:17, "Do not think that I came to destroy the Law or the Prophets. I did not come to destroy but to fulfill." The Levitical law prohibited homosexuality in Leviticus 18:22: "You shall not lie with a male as with a woman. It is an abomination." It also addressed transgenderism in Deuteronomy 22:5: "A woman shall not wear anything that pertains to a man, nor shall a man put on a woman's garment, for all who do so are an abomination to the Lord your God." The teachings of Jesus never abrogated or replaced the moral content of the Mosaic Law. He never gave a new law or modified an existing law. He always explained the true significance of the moral intent of the law, and He fulfilled it perfectly by living out every moral aspect of it. He guided and encouraged us to do the same. He made this clear in Matthew 19:1–6 when He declared that marriage was between one man and one woman and that male and female were the only two genders that God created.

The idea that one's self-perception determines gender identity is a concept influenced by fallen human nature (Eph. 4:17–18). Transgenderism is man's attempt to make his or her biological gender different from how God created them. As explained above, Jesus would undoubtedly call transgenderism a sin. However, as Christians, we must never forget that "all have sinned and fallen short of the glory of God" (Rom. 3:23). We are not called to judge those who may be confused about their gender but instead be willing to receive them with compassion. The Southern Baptist Convention adopted a resolution on transgendered identity as follows:

> We must extend compassion and love to
> those whose sexual self-understanding is shaped
> by distressing conflict between their biological
> sex and their gender identity; to invite our trans-
> gendered persons to trust in Christ and to expe-
> rience renewal in the Gospel [1 Tim. 1:15–16],
> to welcome them into our churches, and as they
> repent and believe in Christ, receive them into

membership [2 Cor. 5:18–20; Gal. 5:14]; and, to oppose all cultural and governing efforts to validate transgender identity as morally praiseworthy [Isa. 5:20].[41]

The Catholic Church has taken a similar position that emphasizes compassion toward the transgendered while cautioning Catholics about "denying the very essence of the human creature through manipulating their God-given gender to suit sexual choices."[42]

When we give ourselves fully to the love of Christ and allow him to have his way in us, we are conformed more and more into the image of God. When facing confusing issues like transgenderism, Christians can seek guidance from the authority of the Bible, the teachings of Jesus, and the Spirit that dwells in each of us. Biblical Christianity must present itself as both a lover of people and a lover of the truth. When we do so, we glorify God. To abandon love is to succumb to hate, and to abandon truth is to believe a lie.[43]

Sarah and Jeff were relieved when the school year ended, and they could focus their full attention on Sam. Now that his parents knew about his desire to be a girl, Sam was becoming more vigilant about his desire to go public about his decision and begin living that way. He was empowered by the Internet which was in no short supply of information on "what to do to change your sex." Under the guise of helping Sam better understand the process, Sarah and Jeff got him to agree to a series of weekly meetings with both Pastor Carl at Mountain View as well as with Dr. Thompson, a psychiatrist and noted specialist on child gender identity issues. Sarah and Jeff had met with Dr. Thompson, a Christian who advocated several therapies and methods to help someone like Sam understand their God-given identity.

Over the next six weeks, the regular meetings with Pastor Carl and Dr. Thompson did not go well. Sam attended but was close-minded to both. Despite their best efforts to speak biblical and scientific truth with him, he became more hostile. Unbeknownst to Sarah and Jeff, Sam registered for the state junior tennis tournament as Samantha Rhodes in the fourteen-year-old *girls'* division. The state had recently passed a law, AB 1266, commonly referred to as the Bathroom Choice Bill. One of the law's provisions allowed individuals to compete in state-sanctioned athletic competitions in the "gender they identify with." Sam had researched the law on the Internet and was confident that the tournament officials could not prevent him from competing in the girls' division.

One day, Sarah was going through the mail and came across an envelope addressed to Samantha Rhodes. She thought it was junk mail until she opened it and surprisingly found a registration confirmation for the tennis tournament. When Sarah and Jeff confronted Sam and, in no uncertain terms, told him they would not permit him to play, he stormed out of the house. Everything came to a head when a week later, Sarah found Sam unconscious in his room as he had taken a large quantity of pills. He was rushed to the hospital and fortunately doctors were able to save him. The suicide note Sarah and Jeff later found was heart-wrenching as Sam conveyed his feelings of abandonment by God and his parents. As part of the hospital's protocol for all suicide attempts, Sam was required to meet with mental health experts. Over the subsequent weeks, Sarah and Jeff prayerfully struggled with the potential loss of their child. They finally decided to support Sam's choice to become a girl and shared the same with him/her.

Sarah and Jeff met with Pastor Carl to share the decision with them. He expressed his disappointment and felt that they should be more patient to allow God and the counselors like him to help Sam understand and realize the truth of his God-given identity. Sarah and Jeff tried to explain the anguish they were experiencing on a daily basis, but Pastor Carl analogized the situation to a couple fighting to save their marriage. God requires perseverance. He said they needed to stay in the fight as Sam's eternal soul was at stake. He closed their meeting in prayer which included a request to God "to help them reconsider their decision." They did not feel very comforted as they left that meeting. They were emotionally drained and felt they were not prepared to "fight or persevere" any longer.

Life was very confusing for the Rhodes family as the summer progressed. They decided to take a family vacation to get away, but it was a difficult adjustment, even as they enjoyed time together. When a family member forgot to address Samantha by her new name, she would get upset, affecting everyone. They planned to go to the beach one day when Samantha insisted on wearing a one-piece girls' swimsuit. An argument ensued, and eventually, they compromised on a T-shirt and shorts. Sarah and Jeff knew they were in for a long road of challenges, and when they returned home from their trip, they asked Samantha to meet with a counselor to help them with transition issues. She agreed.

Andrew was doing his best to be a friend to Jeff, but he, too, was challenged by their decision to allow Sam to proceed with changing his identity. He believed the truth of the Bible, but he was conflicted as he also knew that Scripture called him to "love [his] neighbor as [him]self" (Matt. 22:39). He prayed for the Rhodes family often. When they periodically met, he did his best to talk about other subjects, but their conversations were always awkward. Andrew saw Jeff at the grocery store one weekday evening, and as they left, they agreed to talk further at the upcoming weekend's junior tennis tournament. Jeff did not share that Samantha would compete as a girl in the tournament.

Andrew's fourteen-year-old daughter, Becky, was an excellent tennis player and had won a few competitive tournaments earlier in the year. This weekend was a big event as boys and girls from all over the state traveled to compete in this end-of-summer tournament before the start of the new school year. When they arrived at the tournament and received a copy of the bracket comprised of sixteen girls in the thirteen- to fourteen-age division, they noticed the name Samantha Rhodes. When Andrew saw Jeff a few days earlier, he failed to mention that Sam would be playing in the girls' division as Samantha and competing against Becky. He was visibly confused and upset.

Becky played well as she easily won her first several matches. However, everyone's attention was centered on Samantha. She also easily won her matches. Every court she played on was packed with people watching, and it was not hard to hear the constant muttering about the boy turned girl playing in the tournament. Andrew watched from afar, and although he saw Jeff from a distance, he decided not to talk to him. Late on Sunday afternoon, Becky and Samantha met in the finals. The match was not competitive as Samantha's natural power overwhelmed Becky in a convincing 6-0, 6-0 victory. Becky was heartbroken by what she felt was an unfair match. Andrew tried to console her, but he, too, was upset and struggled with what just happened.

A few days later, Andrew called the varsity girls' tennis coach at the local public high school that Becky would be attending. He was at the junior tournament the past weekend, so he was well aware of the controversy surrounding Samantha. In preparation for the start of school, he had already met with the principal who confirmed that under the new state law, the school was mandated to allow Samantha to play on the girls' tennis team. The school was preparing to make the appropriate physical and logistical accommodations to comply with the law. Andrew was growing increasingly frustrated and reached out to Jeff for a meeting.

When they sat down for coffee, Andrew began with a soft apology for not connecting as promised at the tournament. He offered as an excuse a work crisis that had him occupied on the phone for most of the weekend except during Becky's matches. Andrew shared his concerns over how "aggressively" Sarah and Jeff were transitioning Sam to Samantha. He added that what happened at the tournament was an "embarrassment" to girls' tennis and a significant threat to all youth sports. Jeff calmly responded that they had sought professional guidance and prayerfully were doing their best with each decision, including the one they made allowing Samantha to compete in the girls' division. Jeff confirmed that he had also spoken to the girls' tennis coach at the public high school, and they intended for Samantha to play on the team. Andrew sharply responded that "he did not know what God they were praying to but, in no way, would the God of the Bible be guiding them this way." Andrew continued with more criticism, and Jeff was at a loss to respond. They left the coffee house, not knowing at the time that they would not talk to or see each other again for over nine months.

Andrew organized a meeting with several parents of Becky's friends who would be starting high school with her. A few of them had daughters who played tennis. They all expressed their frustration with the Rhodeses' decision. That meeting lead to several other meetings, including a trip to the state capitol to meet with local legislators regarding the law. Division was growing in the community as several supported the Rhodes family, but many others opposed them. The vast majority in the church were confused and unsure how to respond to an issue they never thought they would have to face in their own community. The church was not providing any real leadership or guidance.

Andrew and Becky decided to enroll at the private high school and avoid the growing controversy and likely circus at the public school. As daily life continued to be challenging for every member of the Rhodes family, especially Samantha, Sarah and Jeff decided to move the family to the other side of town. The kids would still attend the same schools, but a new neighborhood gave them a chance for a fresh start. They felt less and less comfortable at Mountain View and met with the senior pastor at Bethany Church who welcomed them with open arms. With a new home and a new church, they moved forward the best they could.

The importance of Christian unity is clearly stated in the following prayer of Jesus:

> I do not pray for these alone, but also for those who will believe in Me through their word; that they may all be one, as You, Father, are in Me, and I in You; that they also may be one in Us, that the world may believe that You sent Me. And the glory which You gave Me I have given them, that they may be one just as We are one; I in them, and You in Me; that they may be made perfect in one, and that the world may know that You have sent Me, and have loved them as You have loved Me. (John 17:20–23)

In a time when Christians have been divided like never before, Jesus's cry for unity is the very cry of God himself. We have forgotten that our primary duty to other believers is to love them (Rom. 13:8). Our divisiveness grieves God and has a negative impact on an unbelieving world. Jesus suffered and died to unite us with the Father and with each other. The world observes our disunity. It is not only unattractive but also makes us dysfunctional.[44] If our mission is to bring an unbelieving world to know and accept Jesus, we must realize that we need each other and be committed to unity.

> Our divisiveness grieves God and has a negative impact on an unbelieving world.

Chapter 2 outlined the reasons why Christians must honor the absolute truth of the Bible. True Christians are people who acknowledge and live under the Word of God. Doctrinal agreement and unity on the Gospel as outlined in 1 Corinthians 15:1–8 is a must. Any deviations or distortions should not and cannot be tolerated. In Galatians 1:8, Paul declared that "if we, or an angel from heaven, preach any other gospel to you than what we have preached to you, let him be accursed."

In 2 John 7–11, believers are warned that there are "deceivers" who will be spreading their false teachings. John is speaking of the extreme and specific case of people who denied that Christ came in the flesh. The following are a few of the false teachings warned against in the New Testament:

- Claiming "I am the Christ" (Matt. 24:5)
- Calling "Jesus accursed" (1 Cor. 12:3)
- Getting caught up in "myths and endless genealogies [which] promote controversial speculations" (1 Tim. 1:4 NIV)
- Forbidding marriage and certain foods (1 Tim. 4:3)
- Denying that Jesus came in the flesh (1 John 4:1–3; 2 John 7)

- "Turn[ing] the grace of our God into lewdness and deny[ing] the only Lord God and our Lord Jesus Christ" (Jude 4)[45]

The similarity in all of these scriptures is that they focus on key Gospel truths consistent with Paul's instruction in 1 Corinthians 2:2: "Not to know anything among you except Jesus Christ and Him crucified." Over time, however, the biblical category of "false teacher" has been expanded to include anyone who disagrees with us on any theological position or, for that matter, who disagrees with us on anything. This has resulted in huge divisions in the church as evidenced by the thousands of denominations, each believing their theology or methodology is superior.

We need to be firm on truth. We need to believe that God's Word remains unchanged and that it retains all of its power, protection, promise, and peace. We are permitted to challenge each other on teachings, but we must do so with love and humility, seeking their repentance.[46] Loving confrontation and loving correction of truth are both embedded in unity. Christians should not claim to have unlimited or perfect knowledge about God or humanity. However, because the core of our faith is absolutely true, Christians have nothing to fear and should be open to intellectual engagement with fellow believers and non-Christians alike.

In Matthew 4:19, Jesus instructed Peter and Andrew, "Follow Me, and I will make you fishers of men." Jesus's ministry began with a simple call for us to partner with him in spreading the Gospel. Unfortunately, we have added to this Gospel by taking it upon ourselves to not just be "fishers of men" but "cleaners of fish." This is God's job, not ours. We must trust God to speak directly to the broken (transgender, racist, atheist, or any other category) through His Holy Spirit that can bring about change in their heart, mind, and Spirit. Unity does not require us to compromise on our convictions. We are called to help "turn a sinner from the error of his way" (James 5:20). However, our role in the partnership with God is not to change the other person. God has provided us a way to defend the truth in love and allow God the Father, God the Son, and God the Spirit to do the transforming work that only they can do.

Andrew's heart was stirring as it got closer to the retreat. The night before they were scheduled to leave, he received an email from Mountain View's senior pastor, Philip, asking if he could catch a ride to the retreat as his car was in the shop. He lived just a few blocks away, so Andrew and Tommy planned to pick him up on Friday at noon. During the two-hour drive to Shady Woods, Andrew shared the story of the previous summer and his broken friendship with Jeff. Pastor Philip recalled the first meeting he had with Andrew, Pastor Carl, Jeff, and Sarah. Following that meeting, Pastor Carl took over working with the family. Pastor Philip was saddened to hear how things ended, and he was upset with himself for not taking a more active role in pastoring the family through this difficult time. However, he reminded Andrew that we serve a mighty God who can restore broken relationships.

Pastor Philip shared that in Romans 14:18–19, Paul reminded Christians that "he who serves Christ in these things is acceptable to God and approved by men. Therefore let us pursue the things which make for peace and the things by which one may edify another." The goal is peace and edification. Too often, we let our goal slip to correctness and exclusion.[47] Unity requires us to prayerfully work in the Spirit through disagreements and, through love, seek resolution. The Christian life is not easy, especially in a world that is turning the truth upside down. Unity begins by loving the people who stand in front of us, those with whom we are in closest relationship and building unity with them. In love, relationship after relationship can be strengthened and unity will grow. This is a snapshot of heaven where everyone is in complete unity.

> Unity requires us to prayerfully work in the Spirit through disagreements and, through love, seek resolutions.

As they continued their drive up the mountain, Pastor Philip sensed that Andrew was also feeling guilt and shame for abandoning his friend and for his part in allowing the issue to divide the community. He reminded Andrew of how much God has forgiven each of us and, by grace, He gives us the gift of forgiveness to reconcile broken relationships.

> Bearing with one another, and forgiving one another, if anyone has a complaint against another; even as Christ forgave you, so you must also do. (Col. 3:13)

Forgiveness is a decision to call on God to change our hearts. It is a decision that requires us to forgive ourselves for mistakes we have made as well as forgiving others for harm known or unknown that may have impacted us. Forgiveness removes the obstruction or barrier standing between the relationship. With this obstacle removed, the individuals have an opportunity to repair the relationship. The Bible calls this "reconciliation," a process involving a change of attitude that leads to a change in the relationship.[48] To be reconciled means to replace hostility and separation with peace and friendship.[49] Jesus instructed Christians to do this when he said, "Go and be reconciled to your brother" (Matt. 5:24 CSB).

During the reconciliation process, God helps you and the other person work through your differences so that you may discover a new respect and appreciation for each other. When reconciliation is pursued in thought (replacing negative thoughts or memories of the past with positive thoughts or memories), word (expressing kind and affirming words to the other person), and deed (loving actions toward one another), the relationship has an excellent chance of being fully restored and even strengthened. Forgiveness and reconciliation require time, persistence, and patience. We cannot do this in our own strength and wisdom but only through our reliance on God. Reconciliation provides us an opportunity to demonstrate the love and power of God in our lives.

By the time they pulled up to Shady Woods, the discussion with Pastor Philip had energized Andrew, and he was excited at the opportunity to meet with Jeff. However, he was also apprehensive for exactly what to say. Pastor Philip encouraged him to pray about it and trust that the Holy Spirit would guide both him and Jeff when they meet. Bethany Church was housed on the other side of the camp complex. The agenda for the weekend called for two joint activities between Mountain View and Bethany: the Mancathalon (a fun competition in various sporting events) and the final worship service on Saturday night. Andrew was not certain if Jeff was even a part of the Bethany group, but he began to pray and prepare for a potential meeting.

Andrew and Tommy enjoyed the opening afternoon and evening filled with great spiritual activities, delicious food, and an amazing worship band. The next morning began with a devotional and a cabin prayer breakout session, and after lunch, they began to get ready for the Mancathalon. Andrew continued to feel some anxiety about an initial encounter with Jeff and precisely what he would say. When they arrived at the athletic area, Bethany had two teams entered in the Mancathalon, but Andrew did not see Jeff on either team or even in the group from Bethany watching the event. He assumed Jeff was not at the retreat, and he began to relax and enjoyed his time with Tommy. When they returned to the cabin, one of the pastors asked Andrew if he could help the setup team for the big evening worship service. Andrew left dinner early and headed over to the worship center.

As he turned through the woods onto the path leading to the worship center, he saw someone approaching from the other direction. As the person got closer, Andrew could make out that it was Jeff, and as they closed in, they both recognized each other. They slowed their pace down until they were standing face-to-face. Andrew extended his hand, and Jeff accepted with a firm handshake.

The awkwardness of the moment was palpable, but Andrew spoke the first words, "I had prayed you would be here tonight."

This caught Jeff by surprise and seemed to relieve any tension. They walked and talked, mostly exchanging pleasantries about the retreat, but Andrew felt the Spirit leading him to initiate the forgiveness process. He asked Jeff if they could sit down to talk, and they found a quiet spot in the worship center.

Andrew began with a sincere apology and request for forgiveness. Over the next thirty minutes, they proceeded to have a powerful and Spirit-led discussion in which both expressed the challenging emotions they experienced the previous summer. Jeff offered his own apology for not giving Andrew advance notice of Samantha's entry in the tennis tournament. A weight was lifted from both of their shoulders as the discussion progressed. They agreed to meet again when they returned home, and they exchanged a warm embrace as their respective church leaders called each to help set up for the event.

Pastor Philip, who had noticed Andrew and Jeff talking, approached Andrew to see how he was doing. Andrew shared about their conversation and that he was encouraged that he and Jeff had taken the initial steps to restore their relationship. However, Andrew also shared that he felt compelled to share the more significant message of Christian unity with others. Pastor Philip asked him to wait for a minute, and he left to speak to his friend, Lewis, the senior pastor at Bethany. When Pastor Philip returned, he asked if Andrew would like an opportunity to share a few thoughts at the worship event that was scheduled to start in thirty minutes. At first, Andrew hesitated, but the Spirit nudged him to accept the invitation.

Andrew sat anxiously in the audience with Tommy, trying to enjoy the worship music. As Pastor Philip and Pastor Lewis came up on stage for the message, they shared a story of the divided church and how that grieves God. Unity is possible, but it requires every Christian to humble themselves in the Spirit to make that happen. Without humility, we will never have unity.[50] More importantly, without humility, we cannot be in a right relationship with God.[51] They invited Andrew up to the stage.

Andrew confidently began with a powerful statement on why unity should be of utmost importance to every Christian. In his desire to defend a theological position, he arrogantly and callously disregarded a friend. This saddened God. He found Jeff in the audience, turned in his direction, and once again apologized and asked for his forgiveness. God commands us to grow our theology, holiness, and unity simultaneously, not separately, and this is done through love. Our divisions aren't usually caused by a difference in theology but by a lack of relationship.[52] Our problem is not our difference of opinion or interpretation; it's the shallowness of our love.

> Our problem is not our difference of opinion or interpretation; it's the shallowness of our love.

Love is the guiding force to sustain healthy relationships. Jesus commanded us to love each other as Christ loved us (1 John 4:11). God wants every word to be spoken in love. Every sentence at every level of interaction should be spoken in love, leading to greater unity.[53] If there is true love in a Christian relationship and both individuals are committed to the relationship, then a theological disagreement, except for false beliefs renouncing Jesus, does not warrant separation. Instead, when we pursue unity, we demonstrate our love for God, and His love flows from us to all those around us. This kind of unity can inspire a broken and unbelieving world to accept and follow Jesus. As Andrew left the stage, he noticed Jeff wiping tears from his face. He was confident that the healing process would continue for both.

Over the next several weeks, Andrew and Jeff met often. Jeff and Sarah continued to struggle and were challenged by the everyday issues with Samantha. However, they now had another friend praying for them and supporting them. Andrew invited Jeff to join a Bible study made up of men throughout the community. Pastor Philip and Pastor Lewis each took the opportunity to build off what happened at Shady Woods to message to their respective congregations on truth and unity. The men's ministries at both churches began planning for more joint events after the retreat's success. While there continued to be theological differences that were vigorously debated in both churches, the Body of Christ was loving each other well and slowly coming together in unity. God was pleased. Amen.

CONCLUSION

When God first gave me the vision for this book, I had developed a few basic concepts centered on the major theme/title, *Loving through Conflict*. As I researched the issues further, I prayed that He would shine His wisdom on this important subject. I am grateful He did. While my original outline emphasized that love is the necessary virtue by which a relationship can manage conflict well, God revealed to me so much more about love and relationships and what He desires and demands from us as Christians. Our relationship with Him and our relationships with each other may be the single most important thing to God because it both brings Him glory and draws the unbelieving world one step closer to Him.

At the time of creation, God's relationship plan was very simple. He had perfect love with us and gave us the ability to have perfect love with each other. Even though Adam and Eve were unique and different, God designed their relationship to be without conflict. Relationships were perfect. But only for a very short time. The fall and introduction of sin not only impaired our relationship with God but also impaired our relationships with each other. The relational simplicity in God's original plan was turned on its head. Relationships became very complex. Two different people, both uniquely created in God's image, bring to the relationship different values, beliefs, attitudes, and desires cultivated over years of life experience. We are Christians, but we are very different. Unfortunately, our sin nature and inherent selfishness fuel competing interests in our relationships. Conflict is inevitable. We know God will restore everything to perfection when Jesus returns. Until then, how can Christians, living in a fallen world, improve our relationship with Him and with each other? When we encounter conflict, how can we repair damaged or broken relationships? We can only do so through love. God's overflowing love.

God's love is selfless. It guides us to seek the interest of others. When we imitate God's love, we are humble, merciful, forgiving, and compassionate. God's love helps us communicate well with openness toward others. Love provides spiritual protection against the enemy who desires to destroy our relationships. God's love allows us to be honest with each other. Jesus is love. Love and truth are fused together. Love is relationship glue.

So as I reflect back on that fall day described in the "Introduction" in which I observed conflict around every corner, my initial discouragement has turned to hope. In each and every one of those conflicts, I now have hope for those relationships. As Christians love each other well with commitment and perseverance, many of the types of conflicts illustrated will be avoided. When the strongest relationship experiences conflict, love can preserve, redefine, and strengthen the relationship, even if the underlying issue that caused the conflict is not resolved. God's desire—His will for us—is to be in an intimate relationship with Him and intimate relationships with each other. In the Lord's Prayer, we ask, "Your kingdom come. Your will be done on earth as it is in Heaven" (Matt. 6:10). I offer the following prayer for each of you:

Father God,

> We love you and give you praise. Thank you for uniquely making us in your image and for blessing us with an intimate relationship with you and with so many amazing people in our lives. We are sorry for the times that we have not loved others the same way you love us. We are sorry for the conflicts that we have caused and

for any unforgiveness that has added to disunity with our Christian brothers and sisters. Please forgive us. Please fill us with your Spirit so we can love others well. We desire for your love to overflow through us to others. Give us the strength to be obedient to Jesus's teachings and every day make Him Lord of our lives. Please continue to encourage us as Christians to seek unity, the same unity that binds You, Jesus, and the Holy Spirit. In the name of your son, Amen.

STUDY GUIDE

Study 1—The Anatomy of Conflict

Purpose:

To understand the sources of human conflict.

Discussion questions:

1. What is the prominent theme in the secular definition of conflict?
2. How does the biblical view of conflict compare against the secular definition?
3. What were some of the issues that caused the conflict between Paul and Barnabas as described in Acts 15:36–41?
4. Describe a time when sinful attitudes or behaviors caused conflict in your life.
5. How can miscommunication cause unintended conflict?
6. What are some of the current progressive movements causing conflicts in your church or Christian community?

Summary question:

Why is God not surprised by human conflict?

Personal application:

What activities or people are sources of conflict in your life?

Study 2—God's View of Conflict

Purpose:

To understand how God views conflict.

Discussion questions:

1. Why did the apostle Paul in his letter to the Ephesians (chapter 4) emphasize unity?
2. How does Christian diversity contribute to unity?
3. What is the one area where God demands uniformity among Christians? Why?
4. How does our behavior in a conflict provide us with an opportunity to imitate God's love (Eph. 5:1–2) and glorify Him (1 Cor. 10:31)?
5. Describe the four areas in which God wants us to imitate His love when we face a conflict.
6. How did David glorify God in his conflict with Saul in 1 Samuel 24?

Summary question:

How can we please God through our behavior during conflicts?

Personal application:

How are you including God in understanding the conflicts in your life?

Study 3—The Importance of Relationship

Purpose:

To understand the importance of relationship.

Discussion questions:

1. Describe the characteristics of David and Jonathan's close relationship as illustrated in 1 Samuel 18 and 2 Samuel 1?
2. How does your relationship with God impact your relationship with others?
3. Explain the difference between knowledge of God (knowing God) and knowledge about Him.
4. What are the external signs evident in a Christian who knows God?
5. What does it mean to commit to making Jesus Lord of your life?
6. Explain the principle of "love overflow" and how that impacts our relationships.

Summary question:

Why is love the foundation to our relationship with God and others?

Personal application:

How can you grow your knowledge of God and Jesus to strengthen your most important relationships?

Study 4—Relationship Disciplines

Purpose:

To understand the fundamental principles taught and modeled by Jesus that are critical to healthy relationships.

Discussion questions:

1. What are some tools of effective communication that enable us to connect at a deeper level in our relationships?
2. Why is it critical for truth and love to be fused together in our relationships?
3. Explain how openness/transparency, despite being difficult in practice, can improve our relationships.
4. Describe ways you can be sensitive to the emotional and spiritual health of those you are in relationship with.
5. Why is God trustworthy?
6. Why do God and Jesus command respect in our relationships?

Summary question:

Why are relationship disciplines so important when facing a conflict?

Personal application:

Which relationship disciplines do you do well? Which disciplines do you need God's help to strengthen? Why?

Study 5—Conflict Creator—the Enemy

Purpose:

To understand the spiritual forces that can create conflicts and are opposed to healthy relationships.

Discussion questions:

1. How can we be more aware of the temptations of the world and the potential negative influence they have on our relationships?
2. How does our sinful nature carry into our relationships and potentially cause conflicts?
3. As you read and meditate on 1 Peter 5:8, describe how you are being sober and vigilant against the enemy's attack on your relationships?
4. How does the battle between the flesh and will as described by the apostle Paul in Romans 7 potentially lead us to conflicts in our relationships?
5. How are you using the spiritual protection of the armor of God (Eph. 6:10–18) to defend against the enemy's attack on your relationships?
6. What parts of Chris and Julie's story impacted you?

Summary question:

Why is a healthy understanding of spiritual darkness so important in preparing us for potential conflicts in our relationships?

Personal application:

Which relationships in your life are most vulnerable to attacks from the enemy?

Study 6—Resolving a Conflict in Love— the Relationship Is Strengthened

Purpose:

To understand how love enables us to balance competing interests and effectively resolve a conflict, thus strengthening the relationship.

Discussion questions:

1. Why is it difficult to follow God's command to "live in peace with each other" (1 Thess. 5:13) when there is so much chaos in the world?
2. Explain the importance of separating personal and material/substantive issues prior to approaching conflict resolution.
3. Give examples of things to consider when preparing to meet with someone with whom you will be working through a conflict resolution.
4. Why is it important to focus on interests instead of outcome?
5. How can love help a Christian to "make the other's case his or her own" and "seek the interest of others" (Phil. 2:4)?
6. What did Jen and Trish do well to help them resolve their conflict?

Summary question:

Why does a Biblical approach to conflict resolution strengthen a relationship regardless of the outcome?

Personal application:

What changes do you need to make to approach a conflict resolution as a cooperative process instead of a competitive negotiation?

Study 7—Conflict Impasse—Love Preserves the Relationships

Purpose:

To understand how to preserve a relationship that is at a conflict impasse and how to glorify God in the process.

Discussion questions:

1. Explain why the two love commandments in Matthew 22:37–39 describe love as an action and not as an emotion.
2. What does it mean that the "kingdom of God" is here and now?
3. Why is it important to distinguish between major and minor doctrine in our relationships with other Christians?
4. What is God's solution for the relationship to move forward when reaching an impasse? Why?
5. Explain how the principles of humility and imitating God can help the parties who are at an impasse?
6. How was Theresa able to balance her strong desire for the lead pastor position against what was best for the kingdom of God?

Summary question:

Why is it important for Christians to strive to preserve their relationships when they reach a conflict impasse?

Personal application:

What lessons have you learned in how to approach a conflict in which your interests are in direct opposition to the other person's interests?

Study 8—Relationships Redefined to Last—Loving with Boundaries

Purpose:

To understand how to lovingly use boundaries to redefine relationships mired in conflicts.

Discussion questions:

1. Why are our closest and most committed relationships often the most challenging?
2. Explain how the concept of freedom operates within boundaries and why establishing boundaries is loving?
3. How does God use boundaries in His relationship with us?
4. Why do boundaries need to be made visible to others and communicated clearly to those we are in relationship with?
5. How can mentors and accountability partners help Christians in conflict establish healthy boundaries?
6. What did Emily do well in developing boundaries and communicating them to Rick? How did Rick's response strengthen their relationship?

Summary question:

How should Christians use boundaries as a spiritual tool to manage conflicts with love?

Personal application:

Are there any relationship conflicts you are currently experiencing that would benefit from establishing healthy boundaries? Describe in detail how you would lovingly implement these boundaries.

Study 9—Forgiveness and Reconciliation—Unifying Love through Conflict

Purpose:

Through the power of forgiveness, we can reconcile relationships damaged by conflict and, in doing so, demonstrate unity as Christians.

Discussion questions:

1. Why is it difficult to follow the command to "love your neighbor as yourself" (Matt. 27:38) when you have an ideological conflict with another Christian?
2. Why does Christian disunity grieve God? Why is unity so important to Him?
3. How can Christians honor the absolute truth of the Bible with love and humility?
4. Explain the differences between our role and God's role in ministering to the broken.
5. What is required for us to forgive and initiate reconciliation in a damaged or broken relationship?
6. How did Andrew and Jeff glorify God in resorting their relationship? How did it help to unify their community?

Summary question:

Why is God so pleased when damaged relationships are restored? Consider Christ's atonement on the cross in your response.

Personal application:

Describe a damaged or broken relationship that you would like to restore. What impact would a reconciliation have on your family or Christian community?

NOTES

1   Merriam-Webster.com Dictionary, s.v. "conflict," accessed on August 15, 2021, https:www.merriam-webster.com/dictionary/conflict.

2   Ken Sande, *The Peacemaker: A Biblical Guide to Resolving Personal Conflict* (Grand Rapids, MI: Baker Books, 2004), 29.

3   Ibid, 30.

4   Merriam-Webster.com Dictionary, s.v. "unity," accessed on August 15, 2021, https:www.merriam-webster.com/dictionary/unity.

5   Ibid.

6   J. I. Packer, *Knowing God* (Downers Grove, IL: Inter Varsity Press, 1973), 115.

7   Merriam-Webster.com Dictionary, s.v. "relationship," accessed on August 15, 2021, https:www.merriam-webster.com/dictionary/relationship.

8   Ibid, 37.

9   Ibid, 27.

10 John MacArthur, *The Gospel According to Jesus* (Grand Rapids, MI: Zondervan, 2008), 38.

11 MacArthur, *The Gospel According to Jesus*, 32.

12 Charles Swindoll, *Christian Life* (Fullerton, CA: Insight for Living, 1987), 104.

13 C. S. Lewis, *The Four Loves* (New York: Harper Collins, 1960), 98.

14 Ibid, 100.

15 Randell Turner, *Relationship Foundations* (Bloomington, IN: WestBow Press, 2021), 32–39.

16 Merriam-Webster.com Dictionary, s.v. "respect," accessed on August 15, 2021, https:www.merriam-webster.com/dictionary/respect.

17 Andrew Lincoln, *World Biblical Commentary*, vol. 42 (Dallas: World Books, 1990), 442–43.

18 H. K. Williams, Excerpt from the "Group Plan" in the "Young People's Service," *The Biblical World*, vol. 53, no. 1 (Chicago, IL: University of Chicago Press, January 1919), p. 81.

19 Sande, *The Peacemaker: A Biblical Guide to Resolving Personal Conflict*, 80.

20 Ibid, 80.

21 Ronda Nissley, "An Amazing Secret of Marriage Success," accessed on August 15, 2021, http://www.encompasscc.org?blog/an-amazing-secret0to-marriage-

success. This article cites research that fewer than one percent of couples who pray together daily end their marriage.

22 Donald Hagner, *World Biblical Commentary*, vol. 33b (Dallas: World Books, 1995), 648.

23 Ibid, 647.

24 Dallas Willard, *Living in Christ's Presence* (Downers Grove, IL: Inter Varsity Press, 2014), 77.

25 Merriam-Webster.com Dictionary, s.v. "impasse," accessed on August 15, 2021, https:www.merriam-webster.com/dictionary/impasse.

26 Usually when people speak about the major and minor doctrines of Scripture, they are referring to those beliefs that are the most important (major) and those which have less importance (minor). Some believers categorize major doctrines as essentials of the faith, while minor doctrines would be considered nonessentials. For example, the deity of Jesus Christ—teaching that Jesus Christ is actually God—would constitute a major doctrine or essential of the faith. An example of minor doctrine or a nonessential of the faith would be whether infants are required to be baptized.

27 Henry Cloud and John Townsend, *Boundaries* (Grand Rapids, MI: Zondervan, 2017), 168.

28 Ibid, 168.

29 Ibid, 168.

30 Ibid, 45.

31 Ibid, 102.

32 Ibid, 102.

33 Ibid, 102.

34 Ibid, 102–103.

35 Ibid, 103.

36 Tony Evans, *Kingdom Man* (Carol Stream, IL: Tyndale House, 2012), 167.

37 Cloud and Townsend, *Boundaries*, 161.

38 Ibid, 161.

39 Stormie Omartian, *The Power of a Praying Husband* (Eugene, OR: Harvest House Publishers, 2014), 24.

40 Cloud and Townsend, *Boundaries*, 92.

41 Southern Baptist Convention, *Resolution 9 on Transgender Identity*: Baltimore, MD, June 10, 2014. Accessed on August 15, 2021, static.coreapps.net/sbc-am2014/dailies/37336f888c85911fd06d0c9cddd24b90.pdf.

42 Congregation for Catholic Education, *Male and Female He Created Them: Towards a Path of Dialogue on the Question of Gender Identity in Education*, Vatican City, 2019. Accessed on August 15, 2021, education.va/content/dam/cec/Documenti/19_0997_INGLESE.pdf.

43 Lucas Miles, *The Christian Left* (Savage, MN: Broad Street Publishers, 2021), 180.

44 Francis Chan, *Until Unity* (Colorado Springs: David C. Cook, 2021), 95.

45 Ibid, 147–148.
46 Ibid, 148.
47 Ibid, 152.
48 Sande, *The Peacemaker: A Biblical Guide to Resolving Personal Conflict*, 219.
49 Ibid, 219.
50 Chan, *Until Unity*, 57.
51 Ibid, 57.
52 Ibid, 138.
53 Ibid, 195.

BIBLIOGRAPHY

Chan, Francis. *Until Unity*. Colorado Springs: David C. Cook, 2021.

Cloud, Henry and John Townsend. *Boundaries*. Grand Rapids, MI: Zondervan, 2017.

Congregation for Catholic Education. *Male and Female He Created Them: Towards a Path of Dialogue on the Question of Gender Identity in Education*. Vatican City, 2019. Accessed August 15, 2021. education.va/contentdam/cec/Documenti/19_0997_INGLESE.pdf.

Evans, Tony. *Kingdom Man*. Carol Stream, IL: Tyndale House, 2012.

Hagner, Donald. *World Biblical Commentary*, vol. 33b. Dallas: World Books, 1995.

Lewis, C. S. *The Four Loves*. New York: Harper Collins, 1960.

Lincoln, Andrew. *World Biblical Commentary*, vol. 42. Dallas: World Books, 1990.

MacArthur, John. *The Gospel According to Jesus*. Grand Rapids, MI: Zondervan, 2008.

Miles, Lucas. *The Christian Left*. Savage, MN: Broad Street Publishers, 2021.

Nissley, Ronda. "An Amazing Secret of Marriage Success." Accessed August 15, 2021. http://www.encompasscc.org?blog/an-amazing-secret0to-marriage-success.

Omartian, Stormie. *The Power of a Praying Husband*. Eugene, OR: Harvest House Publishers, 2014.

Packer, J. I. *Knowing God*. Downers Grove, IL: Inter Varsity Press, 1973.

Sande, Ken. *The Peacemaker: A Biblical Guide to Resolving Personal Conflict*. Grand Rapids, MI: Baker Books, 2004.

Southern Baptist Convention. *Resolution 9: On Transgender Identity*. Baltimore, 2014. Accessed August 15, 2021. static.coreapps.net/sbc-am2014/dailies/37336f888c85911fd06d0c9cddd24b90.pdf

Swindoll, Charles. *Christian Life*. Fullerton, CA: Insight for Christian Living, 1987.

Turner, Randell. *Relationship Foundations*. Bloomington, IN: WestBow Press, 2021.

Willard, Dallas. *Living in Christ's Presence*. Downers Grove, IL: Inter Varsity Press, 2014.

Williams, H. K. Excerpt from the "Group Plan" in the "Young People's Service." *The Biblical World*, vol 53, no. 1. Chicago: University of Chicago Press, 1919.

SCRIPTURE INDEX

ABOUT THE AUTHOR

Ash Narayan, JD, MA, earned his BS in Accounting from Valparaiso University, his JD from Loyola Law School of Los Angeles, and his MA in Theology from Concordia University. Pursuing his passion for education, he rededicated himself to Jesus and began studying God's Word and followed God's calling to help the poor and marginalized become self-sufficient. Applying his legal and business skills, Ash cofounded the Gethsemane Project to partner with churches throughout the world in developing sustainable ministries. Over the past fifteen years, they have successfully built sustainable orphanages, schools, and children's homes in Mexico, Uganda, Sri Lanka, and Haiti as well as a sustainable ranch and school in Cambodia for victims of human trafficking.

After a long business career, Ash transitioned into full-time ministry, coaching men and couples to help them grow healthy Christian relationships. He facilitated workshops and retreats with the nationally acclaimed Relationship Lifeline program and has successfully co-led the Anchored ministry at his home church, Mariners Church in Irvine, California.

Ash works closely with Transforming Families Global Initiative, a ministry that educates, equips, engages, and encourages men and women, enabling them to discover, develop, and deepen healthy, authentic God-given intimacy within all their relationships. Ash and the founder of Transforming Families, Dr. Randell Turner, have coauthored two books, *Transformational Life* and *Relationship Foundations*.

Ash has attended Mariners for over twenty-three years where he has served in numerous leadership roles. He and his wife, Amy, have been married for twenty-four years, and they have two sons (and two dogs).

www.ingramcontent.com/pod-product-compliance
Lightning Source LLC
Chambersburg PA
CBHW031325160726
47993CB00002B/545